D0458348

"Annie McKee's new book reminds us how basic human things we can do with others—like smile, laugh, cry, and innovate—are all a part of positive, purposive relationships. This book should be required reading in health care systems everywhere, which would preclude a lot of mental health and immune disorders while increasing innovation and engagement!"

—**RICHARD BOYATZIS**, Distinguished University Professor, Case Western Reserve University; coauthor, *Primal Leadership*

"McKee addresses one of the most important—really existential—questions of our time: how to be happy at work. She provides readers with evidence-based insights, practices, and tools for helping them develop a mindset and behaviors that will bring their work life into line with their values and infuse it with meaning and purpose. A must-read for every professional who wants to reach their full potential and flourish at work."

—**NICK VAN DAM**, Global Chief Learning Officer and client advisor, McKinsey & Company; visiting professor, University of Pennsylvania and Nyenrode Business University; and coauthor, *You! The Positive Force in Change*

"Leave it to Annie McKee to take on a complex and deeply personal issue— our struggle to find meaning and happiness at work—and provide a commonsense guide to doing this, with her trademark wisdom and warmth."

—**JOHN FRY**, President, Drexel University

"The digital world is redefining the role of a leader. Leaders must help people discover meaning and purpose at work and help colleagues build authentic relationships. They must build a vision that makes people hope for a future that is better than today. At the intersection of hope, purpose, and friendships lies happiness. This book is a primer for leaders of the new world of work."

—**ABHIJIT BHADURI**, social media influencer; digital transformation coach; and author, *The Digital Tsunami*

"When many of us could be working into our eighties, isn't it crucial to be happy at work? In this timely and fascinating book, Annie McKee draws on a lifetime of experience, insight, and wisdom to show the myths and traps that hold us back and what each of us can and must do now to find happiness at work. A crucial book for an era of longevity."

—**LYNDA GRATTON**, Professor of Management Practice, London Business School

"An essential read. This book is no abstract treatise, but rather offers tools and techniques for making work more meaningful and more fulfilling. It shows much more than it tells, inspires more than it lectures, and leaves you with a personal agenda for action. Whether you're the CEO of a big corporation or working in a small organization, there is much to be gained from reading this book."

—**NIGEL PAINE**, leadership, learning, and technology coach; author, *The Learning Challenge*

"Most of us work to live, and we prefer a happy and meaningful workplace. This research-based book integrates positive psychology and neuroscience with engaging storytelling to give us a deeper understanding of how we can own our personal happiness. A must-read for those wanting to refresh or create a path to happiness in work and life."

—**MARTHA SOEHREN**, Chief Talent Development Officer, Comcast Cable

"Most of us spend the majority of our lives at work. Imagine if we were all happy with how we spent that time on the job. Annie McKee's insightful book shows us that we hold the keys to our own happiness—and why happiness is a business driver we should all care about."

—**TONY BINGHAM**, President and CEO, ATD (Association for Talent Development)

HOW TO BE HAPPY AT WORK

HOW TO BE HAPPY AT WORK

The Power of Purpose, Hope, and Friendships

Annie McKee

HARVARD BUSINESS REVIEW PRESS

Boston, Massachusetts

WITHDRAWN

Copyright 2017 Annie McKee
All rights reserved
Printed in the United States of America

10 9 8 7 6 5 4 3 2 1

No part of this publication may be reproduced, stored in or introduced into a retrieval system, or transmitted, in any form, or by any means (electronic, mechanical, photocopying, recording, or otherwise), without the prior permission of the publisher. Requests for permission should be directed to permissions@hbsp.harvard.edu, or mailed to Permissions, Harvard Business School Publishing, 60 Harvard Way, Boston, Massachusetts 02163.

The web addresses referenced in this book were live and correct at the time of the book's publication but may be subject to change.

Library of Congress Cataloging-in-Publication Data
Names: McKee, Annie, 1955- author.
Title: How to be happy at work : the power of purpose, hope and friendships /
   by Annie McKee.
Description: Boston, Massachusetts : Harvard Business Review Press, [2017]
Identifiers: LCCN 2017008391 | ISBN 9781633692251 (hardcover : alk. paper)
Subjects: LCSH: Quality of work life. | Employee motivation. | Happiness. |
   Hope. | Friendship. | Personnel management.
Classification: LCC HD6955 .M365 2017 | DDC 650.1–dc23 LC record
available at https://lccn.loc.gov/2017008391

ISBN: 978-1-63369-225-1
eISBN: 978-1-63369-226-8

The paper used in this publication meets the requirements of the American National Standard for Permanence of Paper for Publications and Documents in Libraries and Archives Z39.48-1992.

This book is dedicated to
Eddy, Rebecca, Sean, Sarah, Andrew, and Benji,
with all my love.
Erin, you are in my heart.

CONTENTS

HOW TO BE HAPPY AT WORK

Life Is Too Short to Be Unhappy at Work

Happiness Is a Choice

Life really is too short to be unhappy at work.

Yet far too many of us aren't even close to being content—much less delighted—with our work or our workplaces. Instead, we are stressed and exhausted. We can't remember what we used to love about our jobs. Colleagues we trust and respect are few and far between, and half the time it doesn't even feel safe to be ourselves. All of this is spilling over into our personal lives. We're having a hard time sleeping or have given up on exercise. Relationships are suffering, too. We feel trapped and struggle to see how things will get better.

No one wants to live like this. Still, a lot of us give up and settle for less-than-fulfilling jobs. We tell ourselves that we're not supposed to be happy at work; that's for other parts of life. We try to cope by avoiding that bad manager or getting that stubborn, annoying person off the team. We shut down, give less, and fantasize about telling someone off. Sometimes we run away from the job, the company, even our careers. But running away isn't going to make things better. To be happy, I've discovered, you've got to run *toward* something: meaningful work; a hopeful, inspiring vision of your future; and good relationships with the people you work with every day.

Happiness at Work: Purpose, Hope, and Friendships

My discoveries about the importance of happiness at work—and what we can do to build and sustain it—come from a lifetime of advising leaders and studying the cultures of major businesses and nongovernmental organizations all over the world. I've always been fascinated to find that rare and special company where people are happy at work. In these companies, people are profoundly engaged, motivated, and committed. In these companies, individuals and the enterprise thrive.

When I joined forces with leaders to help make these companies even better—to create powerful, resonant organizations where people can be and do their very best—we often made headway. Over the years, though, I've been puzzled and dismayed at the sheer number of people who are deeply unhappy at work and how hard it is to reach them. I myself have had periods when I was truly happy and thriving at work and times when I was miserable. What, I wondered, makes the difference? What leads to long-lasting fulfillment at work? What leads to happiness? And can we even expect to be happy at work? Does it really matter?

To answer these questions, I reviewed my work on emotional intelligence and resonant leadership and revisited the dozens of studies I've done in companies worldwide. What I found is both simple and profound: happiness matters at work as much as it does in our personal lives. And when we are happy, we are more successful.

This flies in the face of the myth that we don't have to be happy at work and we shouldn't even expect to be. Luckily, though, we live in a time when organizations and academia are taking happiness seriously. Leaders in major oil companies, provincial governments, technology startups, and media corporations have often told me that happy employees are more creative and committed. My studies of organizational culture and leadership practices in South Africa, Cambodia, Italy, France, Germany, and the United States show the same thing: when we feel deep, abiding enjoyment in what we do, we learn more, see more, and do more.

I was encouraged to dig even more deeply into my work and the wisdom shared by the many people I have had the privilege to work with over the years. I wanted to know what it takes to be happy at work. My conclusion: to be truly happy at work, we need purpose, hope, and friendships.[1]

Happiness Begins with Purpose and Meaningful Work

We are wired to seek meaning in everything we do. It's what makes us human. In some cases, it's what keeps us alive.

In his classic book, *Man's Search for Meaning*, Austrian psychiatrist and holocaust survivor Victor Frankl shows that even in the worst of circumstances, purpose, hope, and connection are what keep us going. True, his story of finding good in evil and pursuing a noble purpose in spite of the horrors of life in concentration camps is nothing short of heroic. Yet, as Frankl so eloquently shows us, we strive to find meaning in our day-to-day lives no matter where we are or what conditions we're subjected to.[2]

As you have probably discovered, you can easily lose sight of what you value and ignore the aspects of yourself that matter most to you, especially when you're struggling with dysfunctional organizations, bad bosses, and stress. You're then likely to put meaning and purpose on the back burner or wait for someone else to give you a compelling reason to love your job. Couple all this with the outdated but pervasive notions that personal values don't belong in the workplace, and you have a recipe for disengagement and unhappiness.

You need conviction to insist on living your purpose at work. As you will see in this book, the effort is worthwhile. Having a sound, clear, and compelling purpose helps you be stronger, more resilient, and able to tap into your knowledge and talents. As you discover which parts of your job are truly fulfilling—and which are soul destroying—you will be in a better position to make good choices about how you spend your time and what you pursue in your career.

Hope's Contribution to Happiness

Like meaning, hope is an essential part of our human experience. This is as true at work as in any corner of our lives. Hope, optimism, and a vision of a future that is better than today help us rise above trials and deal with setbacks. Hope fuels energy, creativity, and resilience. Hope makes it possible to navigate complexity, deal with pressure, prioritize, and make sense of our crazy organizations and work lives. And hope inspires us to reach our potential—something virtually everyone wants for themselves.

Unfortunately, we often assume that our organization's vision is enough to keep us hopeful and focused on the future. I've rarely seen this to be the case. An organization's vision, however inspiring, is for the organization—not you. Even the most noble organizational vision seldom speaks to our most cherished, personal hopes and dreams.

To be truly happy at work, we need to see how our workplace responsibilities and opportunities fit with a *personal* vision of our future. This kind of vision is vitally tied to hope and optimism, which we can, with focus and hard work, cultivate even in difficult jobs and toxic workplaces. When we see our jobs through a positive lens, and when a personal vision is front and center in our minds, we are more likely to learn from challenges and even failures, rather than be destroyed by them. With hope, optimism, and a personal vision, we can actively choose a path toward happiness—a path away from disengagement, cynicism and despair.

Friendships and Happiness at Work

Resonant relationships are at the heart of collective success in our companies. That's because strong, trusting, authentic relationships form the basis for great collaboration and collective success.

But, I've found, we need more than trust and authenticity to get us through good times and bad. We need to feel that people care about us and we want to care for them in return. This, too, is part of our human makeup. We also want to feel as if we are accepted for who we are, and that we work in a group, team, or organization that makes us feel proud and inspires us to give our best effort.

Adding it all up, the kind of relationships we want and need look a lot like friendships. Yet, one of the most pernicious myths in today's organizations is that you don't have to be friends with your coworkers. Common sense and my decades of work with people and companies show the exact opposite. Love and a sense of belonging at work are as necessary as the air we breathe.

Purpose, hope, and friendships don't just appear magically. You need to work for them. You need to engage in mindful self-reflection and be truthful about what you discover. Then you need to *act*. This is where your emotional intelligence comes in.

Emotional Intelligence and Happiness: A Virtuous Circle

We've known for years that emotional intelligence (EI) is key to being effective at work. The more EI you have, the better you are at your job—no matter what kind of role you have or how senior you are.[3] What's clear to me now is that EI also affects your ability to find and sustain happiness.

EI enables conscious reflection and action—that magic combination that keeps you from running from one unhappy situation to the next. In practical terms, EI is a set of competencies that enables you to understand your own and others' feelings, and then use this knowledge to act in ways that support your own and others' effectiveness. Moreover, EI will help you tune in to purpose and hope to establish friendly, resonant relationships at work. Here's how EI links to happiness at work:

- **Self-awareness.** Understanding your own feelings and moods is the first step in recognizing what truly fulfills you, what you find meaningful and exciting at work. Self-awareness also extends to articulating why you feel angry, sad, stressed, motivated, or inspired—more clues about what supports engagement with your work. Cultivating the ability to tune in to your emotions helps you home in on what is most important to you: your values, guiding principles, and overarching life purpose. This is where happiness begins.

- **Self-management and emotional self-control.** Emotionally intelligent people are adept at managing their own feelings, both positive and negative. Managing your emotions is an essential skill that helps you weather the storms that are ever present in our high-pressure workplaces. Self-management enables you to cultivate a positive outlook—to choose to be optimistic even when things are tough. This is the foundation of hope and a personally compelling vision of the future, another foundational component of happiness at work.

- **Empathy.** Empathy is essential for building sound relationships at work and for creating friendships that make you happy. When this skill is activated, you understand others' thoughts and feelings—why they are upset or engaged and passionate about their work. You understand that the relationships between people and on teams are complex, and you don't settle for simplistic explanations for why people behave the way they do. This knowledge equips you to make better decisions about how to engage with people—how to inspire, motivate, and support others to be successful. Empathy also enables you to create strong bonds and esprit de corps. Taking it one step further, empathy allows you to create a resonant microculture in your team—a microculture that is built on mutual respect for one another's dreams and differences, a sense of belonging, commitment to making one another successful, and fun.

Here's a secret about EI: it's a virtuous circle. The more you use it, the better you get. In this book, you will have many opportunities to practice and develop your EI as you deepen your self-awareness around purpose and meaning, engage a more positive outlook and build an inspiring vision for your future, and seek to build friendly relationships with coworkers.

Your Road Map to Happiness at Work

How to Be Happy at Work gives you the information and tools you need to break the unhappiness cycle and to find meaning, hope, and friendships in your daily work. Throughout this book, I will lay out a road map to achieve personal happiness while creating a resonant environment in which others can be happy and effective, too. Along the way, I will present reflective exercises and practical advice for getting back in touch with what's most important to you and improving your work relationships.

In chapter 1, I will define happiness at work and explain the business case, too. Then, in chapter 2, I will talk about common happiness traps—mindsets that keep us stuck and unfulfilled. I will also show how you can use EI to break free from these traps and avoid them in the future.

In the next three chapters, I will explain the essential elements of happiness at work: purpose, hope, and friendships. In chapter 3, I will talk about the power of purpose and how you can find ways to live your values and have positive impact at work no matter what job you have. Through stories and my own experience, I will share practical ways to get in touch with what's important to you and integrate it into your day-to-day activities. You will see that you *can* live your purpose at work, and when you do, you will be happier and more effective—and so will the people around you.

In chapter 4, I will focus on how to build and sustain hope, even when the odds are against you. I will talk about the importance of leaning in to your natural optimism, and how to make sure that your personal vision of the future is your guiding light.

In chapter 5, I will debunk the myth that we should not be friends with people at work. Then, I will discuss what we really do need in our relationships and teams at work: caring, respect, and feeling that we belong.

In chapter 6, I will talk about how to reclaim purpose, hope, and good relationships when you face stress or serious setbacks at work or at home. I'll also explain how to notice life's wake-up calls—those faint whispers that tell you something's not right at work—so you can make course corrections before that wake-up call becomes a jarring alarm. Finally, in chapter 7, I will talk about how you can make others happier at work by creating a resonant microculture in your team, whether you lead it or not. I will explain when and how to create an environment that supports happiness for you and everyone you touch at work.

Throughout the book, I will share stories from managers, executives, and others about the things they do at work that enable them—and those around them—to be happier and more successful. Naturally, there's a lot of research behind the ideas in this book—my own and others'. But this book is not meant to be hidden in an ivy tower. Instead, my goal is to present a practical, evidence-based framework that helps you use your EI to find meaning, hope, and friendships at work.

Happiness at work is a choice. When you decide to look within yourself to connect with what's most important to you, what makes you feel hopeful about the future, and what you long for in your relationships, you are taking that first, all-important step toward a work life that is deeply satisfying, challenging, and fun. With conviction and practice, you can be happy *and* successful— and love your work.

CHAPTER 1

Why Happiness Matters at Work

If You Sacrifice Happiness, You Sacrifice Success

"I'm working harder than ever before . . . and I don't know if it's worth it anymore."

Hearing these words from my friend "Ari" worried me a lot. As senior vice president of sales at a well-respected company, he has signed up time and again for the challenge, and he's delivered quarter after quarter. I've always known him to be an excellent leader: smart, emotionally intelligent, and wise—just the kind of person we want at the top of a company.[1]

Ari's division is doing well. No big crises are on the horizon, other than the now-routine demand to squeeze more profit out of the business. So why is Ari so unhappy that he's thinking of quitting his job? What's causing him to question his entire career and even his worth as a human being? The constant pressure, stress, and never-ending change initiatives are part of it, he told me. He's most definitely sick of the politics on the senior team. And the rat race, he said, has finally gotten to him. Once again, he's going to have to lay off more people, and for what reason? To deliver yet another quarter?

Ari just doesn't see the point anymore, and the ends no longer justify the means. He is demoralized, disillusioned, and burned-out. He feels isolated and alone and has lost sight of what he used to find exciting and meaningful at work. He's given up hope that things will get better. He shows up every day and tries to play the game, but it's getting harder and harder to keep up the charade. In his more honest moments, he admits he's not as good a leader anymore. He's pretty sure others would agree.

Ari's not alone. Many people are sick to death of their jobs. They are resentful and cynical, and they aren't doing themselves—or others—much good. When we live this way for years, we can—and often do—lose interest in the things that we used to like. We avoid people and we have little creativity or energy.

This situation is unacceptable. Most of us work more than eight hours a day. That means that if we are unhappy at work, we are miserable for more than a third of our lives. Time away from our jobs (if there is such a thing) is affected, too, because we don't leave our feelings at the office and unhappiness seeps into the rest of life. Our families and friends suffer when we are disengaged, dissatisfied, and unfulfilled. Worse, slow-burning stress, anger, and other negative emotions can literally kill us.

Destructive emotions like fear and constant frustration interfere with reasoning, adaptability, and resilience. We just can't focus when we're gripped by negativity or when we're obsessing about how to protect ourselves (or get back at our boss). We can't possibly be effective at work—or anywhere else—when we feel this way. Neither can our organizations.[2]

And the other side of the coin? Companies with happy and engaged employees outperform their competition by 20 percent.[3] A growing number of studies in fields like positive psychology and neuroscience show that happiness is conducive to personal effectiveness and success, too.[4] Candice Reimers, a senior manager at a high-tech firm, brought this to light in a conversation we had about how to be happy at work over the long term, even when challenges are many and tensions run high.[5]

Like Ari, Candice works hard and gives a lot of herself to her company and her colleagues. She faces intense pressure, just as Ari does. But Candice isn't questioning the value of her work or her commitment to her job; it's just the opposite. As she put it, "I find meaning and purpose in my work. Work fulfills me because it exposes me to new challenges that my personal life doesn't always provide. My work gives me access to amazing, brilliant people who challenge me to think in different ways." She talked about her work being a way to realize her personal vision while contributing to her company's mission as well. It was clear to me that her job is in line with her passions: what she does at her company is an expression of her values and a way for her to have positive impact on the world.

I wanted to know how Candice was able to manage the stress and retain her positive, inspiring attitude while so many people, like Ari, become disillusioned. When I asked her to help me understand, she told me about a project that could have caused stress and anxiety, but instead was a source of joy.

A few years back, Candice was leading a crucial, visible project that could put her company at the forefront of a new market—if they got it right and made it to market quickly. She found the ambiguity of this new market thrilling and motivating. It was also scary, especially when it became clear that the company's leaders were counting on her team to build new products for internal customers and then quickly—very quickly—launch something externally.

True innovation is always daunting; it was doubly so in this case because of the visibility and pressure. Candice was nervous, naturally, and she knew that any normal person in her position or on her team would have doubts and concerns. Some might even feel that failure could cost them their jobs. But, knowing that fear is not a driver of innovation and stress kills creativity, Candice recognized that her first challenge was to resist the urge to give in to her own worries or team members' doubts. Instead, she concentrated on the exhilaration of the challenge and the thrill that comes from experimenting and solving big problems. She articulated what she saw as the noble purpose of the project: the team wasn't just positioning the company in a new business, it was contributing to a movement that could have positive impact on people around the world. This shared vision enabled team members to feel hopeful and proud of their role as innovators, and they focused on the upside rather than the perils.

Candice made a potentially frightening process rewarding for her team by tapping into the power of purpose. She energized and motivated team members, while painting an exciting and hopeful view of the future. She fostered a "we're in this together" mindset that made people feel they belonged to an important group, one with a resonant microculture marked by excitement, enthusiasm, safety, and trust—the kind of environment where people can take big risks and have fun without the fear of losing their jobs. In this kind of team, people celebrate creativity and enjoy even routine daily activities. They want to help one another succeed.

Team members worked hard and they worked well together. The project benefited from the positive energy that traveled from one person to the next and the friendships that grew as people learned together. As Candice put it, "It was new, uncharted territory and I felt like we were all explorers just trying to figure this out together. We were sharing articles, doing research, bringing new knowledge back, making some mistakes, and fixing those mistakes. And, we shared our mistakes with other teams who were using the tools we were creating. We learned. And, we launched on time and successfully."

Candice and Ari: Finding the Path to Happiness at Work

Most of us are not nearly as miserable as Ari, and perhaps not as consistently inspired and motivated as Candice. Ari still has moments when he finds joy in what he does and remembers the high points in his career. But by looking at how they each approach their jobs, we can begin to see how to improve our own happiness at work.

Candice and Ari are both highly intelligent, ethical people who want the best for the people they care about at work and at home. They've both been successful in a variety of work situations (Ari was a management consultant; Candice has worked in a variety of industries in the United States and abroad). Both care about their work and their organizations.

But Candice had what Ari had lost: clarity about the value of her work, an inspiring vision of the future, and resonant relationships. Candice's approach to the innovation project defines what it means to stay on the right side of the happiness line.[6] She actively chose to see the upside, not the threats. She focused on an inspiring, meaningful purpose and encouraged people to work well together and have fun. This is how she works in general. Naturally, she has her bad days, weeks, even months. We all do. But she manages to stay engaged and happy most of the time.

With dedicated effort, Ari found his way, and he did not quit his job. The first step was accepting that he deserved to be happy at work (for some of us, this is a big step). Then, he focused on recapturing what was most important to him in life and learning how to bring it back to work. Over time, he rediscovered what he loved about his job—what made it feel meaningful and important. He rebuilt bridges and reconnected with people he used to like and trust at work. He also began to see what he wanted next. He surprised himself with this discovery: what he wanted, it turned out, wasn't that CEO job. He wanted to lead the new division that just might keep the company at the forefront of the industry as technology redefined the business. Ultimately, he rediscovered what it means to be happy at work.

Defining Happiness at Work

I define happiness at work as a *deep and abiding enjoyment of daily activities fueled by passion for a meaningful purpose, a hopeful view of the future, and true friendships.*[7] I stand firmly in the belief that happiness is possible for everyone. Moreover, happiness is a human right.

Happiness is not simply about feeling good in the moment. That is hedonism. True, happiness includes experiences and feelings like joy and excitement, pleasure, and a sense of overall well-being. But that's not all. Happiness is also linked with attitudes and behaviors like finding our calling, altruism, empathy, contributing, and giving back.[8]

Depending on the era, the culture, and the times, happiness has been linked with self-sacrifice, honesty, morality, loyalty, and a host of other values and human experiences. Most of the world's major religions and philosophers attend to happiness, of course.[9]

And, what it means to be happy and who deserves it permeates politics, mainstream media, and the business press, too.[10]

We have thousands of years of wisdom around happiness that is now being applied to what we do at work and how our companies and institutions function.[11] For my part, I have conducted field research and interviewed everyone from the janitor to the CEO in organizations all over the world. Through these conversations, I have learned the obvious truth: happiness is vitally important in the workplace. When our work has meaning, when we see an enticing vision of the future, and when we have strong, warm relationships, we are emotionally, intellectually, and physically equipped to do our best.

Emotions, Happiness, and Resonance at Work

Daniel Goleman, Richard Boyatzis, and I have been in the trenches for years, studying how our feelings, moods, and actions have impact on our experience and success at work. What we've found is that positive emotions—like those we experience when we are happy—support individual and collective success.[12] Our research goes hand in hand with rapid advances in positive psychology and neuroscience. In both arenas, there's a growing body of scientific evidence that shows how profoundly emotions influence our thoughts, behaviors, and outcomes.[13]

Most of us intuitively know that feelings and inner experiences like eagerness, enjoyment, optimism, belonging, and confidence fuel our energy and creativity. Similarly, emotional upsets, anger, fear, or cynicism make it hard to excel—or even be average.[14] Think about your own experience at work. When you are stressed to the max, afraid of your manager, or constantly upset with colleagues, what happens? Most of us shut down. Some of us fight. We certainly don't do our best. Over time, we slip into a state where we can't seem to find our way back to happiness, and we're not as effective as we once were. This is what Richard Boyatzis and I call the "sacrifice syndrome."[15]

On the other hand, when we are driven by a sense of purpose, when we feel optimistic and enjoy being with our colleagues, we're better able to access our knowledge, experience, and emotional intelligence. We are more open to new ideas and can more easily tap into our intuition. We are able to process information more quickly and more thoroughly, be creative, and get along with people who are different from ourselves. Simply put, our brains work better when we feel good.

Activate Your Emotional Intelligence

Emotions affect our bodies as well as what we think and do. For this reason, we need to pay attention to our feelings and moods. Sometimes, negative emotions like fear, frustration, and anger signal that something is really wrong. Most times, though, we overemphasize these kinds of feelings in our minds. It helps to examine them and to make a concerted effort to tap into and emphasize the positive emotions that support well-being and effectiveness:

1. It's Sunday afternoon. You're thinking about your upcoming week at work. What's getting your attention? What do you look forward to? What would you rather avoid? Is anything causing you to feel anxious?

2. Focus on something that worries or bothers you about your upcoming week, and also on something you are eager

to do, something that makes you feel excited and happy. Jot a few notes about the feelings that go along with each anticipation. Try to also note *why* you feel as you do.

3. Now, ask yourself: Is it possible for me to focus more on what I am looking forward to at work during the upcoming week and less on what I am anxious about? What's stopping me? What might help me steer my feelings toward positivity?

If you make a habit of examining your workweek like this, you will see that when you are hopeful and plan to enjoy what you're doing, or when you're appropriately challenged to learn and grow, you will improve your ability to use your existing knowledge, adapt your perspective as situations change, and use your emotional intelligence, too.

Emotions are contagious, too. Our feelings have an impact on how others feel and the extent to which *their* brains work. Positive emotions and a state of mind characterized by hope and compassion create a resonant climate, an environment where everyone can be fulfilled and effective, too.[16]

The Business Case: Happiness *before* Success

A common myth tells us that once we achieve success, we'll be happy. If this were true, all successful people would be happy. They are not. I know far too many people who, as they rise or even reach the pinnacle of their careers, are desperately unhappy. In spite of the trappings of wealth and power, they find themselves questioning everything, just as Ari did at the beginning of the chapter. In this state, they rarely maintain true success. At the least, they suboptimize their potential.

The belief that we will be happy once we become successful is backward. It all *starts* with happiness because happiness breeds resonance and resonance breeds success.

Scholars agree, starting with the popular author and psychologist Shawn Achor, who says it in a straightforward, no-nonsense manner: "Happiness comes before success." This statement is based on studies showing that when we are positive, we are 31 percent more productive and 40 percent more likely to receive a promotion, we have 23 percent fewer health-related effects from stress, and our creativity rates triple.[17] As Achor puts it, "When we find and create happiness in our work, we show increased intelligence, creativity, and energy, improving nearly every single business and educational outcome."[18] Stanford researcher Emma Seppälä says it this way: "Happiness . . . has a profound positive effect on our professional and personal lives. It increases our emotional and social intelligence, boosts our productivity, and heightens our influence over peers and colleagues."[19]

These studies support what we know about emotion: it dramatically affects our ability to think and act in the world of work. When we are happy, we are better at what we do. In the end, happy people perform better than their unhappy peers.[20]

So, if we sacrifice happiness, we sacrifice success. Yet in spite of the wealth of research showing that happiness matters at work and that it contributes significantly to our success, many people still do not believe that we can or even should be happy at work—or we get in our own way.

Personal Reflection and Mindful Practice

Defining Happiness for Myself

People often describe happiness in similar ways. But, because we've all had different life experiences, there are key differences in how we define happiness. It's important to know what *you* think it is. Then, you can more easily go after it!

1. What is *my* definition of happiness? Where did my beliefs about happiness come from? What role do family, religion or spirituality, philosophy of life, and experience play in how I define happiness?

2. Does my definition of happiness limit where, when, and with whom I can experience joy, fun, and real fulfillment?

3. Is my way of viewing happiness serving me well? Why, or why not?

4. If I were to redefine what it takes to make me happy at work, what would my new definition be?

An Exercise in Self-Awareness and Choice

Reflecting deeply on our lives and our work is something we often don't find time to do in the midst of our day-to-day activities. This exercise will help you to slow down and to thoughtfully consider what supports you to be happy at work and what gets in the way. As you think about your approach to work, you will increase self-awareness, especially about mindsets and conditions that make you happy.

Think about a time when you really liked your work, when you were truly engaged and loved what you were doing. Now, tell the story of this experience. Start by jotting some notes about the "who, what, where, when" of this situation.

Next, think about what you, the lead actor in the story, were doing, thinking, and feeling during this time. Try to also add a few notes on what was underneath your thoughts, feelings, and actions: What was driving you? What was inspiring, exciting, energizing? What was fun about this situation?

Now, tell another story—a story about a time in your life when work was not fulfilling, when you were unhappy. Jot all the same kinds of notes that you did for your first story.

Look at your stories carefully: What was different about the two experiences? Start with outside yourself: Was there something different about your bosses, your working conditions, your colleagues, how you were treated? Now, look inside: Beyond the obvious positive and negative reactions to each situation, what was different about *you*? What choices did you make in each scenario that might have contributed to your happiness, or lack of it? Try to focus not only on what you did, and how you behaved, but on how you *felt*, too.

What can you learn from your choices about what to think, do, and feel in situations that are good and situations that are not?

CHAPTER 2

The Happiness Traps

Myths That Hold Us Back

I've always wondered why we don't fight back—why we settle for so little happiness at work. I've done this myself a couple of times during my career. It was painful. I even got sick. I've heard bright, self-aware people tell the same story, over and over again. Why do so many of us accept less-than-optimal work experiences?

I've searched organizations all over the world for the answer. I've plumbed my personal work experience in multiple careers and I've asked executives in confidential coaching sessions. I've looked at scholarly studies and my own research at dozens of companies.[1] I've come to three conclusions.

First, we've bought into old myths about the meaning of work and what we can expect from it (or not). Namely, we believe that work isn't supposed to be fun or fulfilling, and that we don't have to like the people we work with. Instead, we're there to follow orders and produce results. Our values, hopes, and dreams have a very small place in this picture.

Second, most of us have stumbled into happiness traps—mindsets and habitual ways of approaching work and career that keep us stuck on a hamster wheel and pursuing the wrong goals.

Third—and this is the good news—there's something we can do to break free from these old myths and dangerous traps: develop and use our emotional intelligence.

In this chapter, I will talk about these myths and the five most common happiness traps. Then, I will discuss what you can *do* about them—how you can rely on and develop your emotional intelligence so you can break free and begin to chart a path to a work life that fits what *you* want.

Happiness: A Dirty Word at Work?

Only one-third of US employees are engaged at work. The rest are either neutral or actively disengaged. They are bored, uninvolved, or ready to sabotage plans, projects, and even other people. The statistics are similar in other countries and regions, and across virtually all sectors and industries. And these dismal figures have remained largely constant over the years despite economic ups and downs.[2]

This makes no sense to me. When we take a job, we usually start out excited by the opportunity to do something meaningful and impactful. We see a personal benefit to the job, we like the company, and we are eager to work with good people to achieve common goals. We expect to enjoy our jobs. In other words, we expect to be engaged and we want to be happy.[3] But that's not how it usually works out.

What happens to us? What's driving us in the wrong direction? I believe the problem starts with age-old beliefs about the nature of work.

Myth One: Work Has to Be Grueling

When our ancestors had to scratch a meager living from the land, when each day was a struggle to survive, work was physically demanding and exhausting. Not every moment brought misery, of course. If you've put your hands in the dirt and watched plants grow or if you've tended cows or goats or chickens, you know the deep and abiding satisfaction that comes from working with the land to feed your family. But it's far from easy. Add inequitable distribution of land, disease, and poor weather conditions and you've got a recipe for illness, helplessness, and sorrow.

As societies industrialized, the notion that work should be painful grew and spread as workers lost autonomy, the joy of seeing the fruits of their labors, and even fresh air. Instead, they found themselves in tedious, physically taxing jobs where they were treated as recalcitrant children who, if given the chance, would slack off. Managers fared slightly better, but they were also cogs in the wheel of a machine that's primary purpose was to generate profit for owners and distant shareholders.

Work today can still be physically demanding and difficult due to constant change, lean organizations, and blurred boundaries between work and the rest of life. We can feel as if we are always working—and sometimes not making enough progress. Over time, this can wear us down.

But we can't simply accept that work has to be hard and painful. If we do, we condemn ourselves to a life of misery—or at least frustration. No human being deserves this. More, if we and our organizations are to be successful, we need to be in a state of mind that helps us think and be effective. We need to be able to use our intellect to innovate and our emotional intelligence to deal with our increasingly diverse global companies. We cannot do this if we experience our work as unpleasant, difficult, and unsatisfying. This leads to the next myth, one that has also grown and spread over many decades.

Myth Two: How We Feel at Work Doesn't Matter

As the twentieth century dawned, the industrial age spawned management consultants like Frederick W. Taylor, who became famous for creating ways to get the most work out of people in the shortest time.[4] His advice was attractive to owners of the coal, steel, and burgeoning automobile companies, who jumped at the chance to maximize efficiency while gaining even more control over workers they did not trust.

Taylor's methods were seen even then as inherently flawed. His measurements of worker output weren't very scientific, nor were they accurate. The programs were also dehumanizing: the goal was to wring as much out of people as possible without killing them. But, in the heyday of the movement to production line manufacturing, the notion that employees could do more with less was so attractive that it caught on everywhere—and well beyond the boundaries of factories.

It wasn't all bad: the pursuit of efficiency and profit was also a driver of change and improvement. For instance, as science showed that better physical space, lighting, and break time improved productivity, working conditions began to improve.

Changes that addressed the psychological needs of employees, however, were slower to emerge despite a growing body of evidence from fields as varied as the military, psychology, and economics. By the middle of the last century, there was a vast body of knowledge showing that how we feel about our bosses, work, and workplaces affects our contributions and outcomes. Common sense tells us the same thing: emotional and social needs don't disappear when we are at work. On the contrary, our feelings and the quality of our relationships have an impact on our overall well-being and success at work, too.

So, the myths that early management consultants like Taylor perpetuated about what aspects of ourselves matter at work are outdated, flawed, and harmful, too. The same goes for another common myth that emerged during the last century—that work is not meant to be a path to fulfillment.

Myth Three: We Can't Ask for More of Work

Fast-forward to the twenty-first century, and you'll recognize more than just the vestiges of Taylor's approach, in an era that is vastly different from that first industrial age. Many of the views that were held then (flawed as they were) still hold sway. For example, there's still the misguided notion that the higher up in the organization you are, the smarter you are. That simply isn't true. Everyone needs to be smart in today's workplace. In addition, shifts in the market and rapid advancements in technology mean we are constantly having to change how we work. We often feel as if the minute we master something, it's time to do it differently.

Add to this the fact that industries like oil and gas, chemical production, publishing, and health care (to name just a few) are undergoing seismic shifts due to more transparency and regulations. This means more changes, many of which we have little or no control over.

This is hard enough, but when we aren't trusted to figure things out for ourselves, we become demoralized. And here's what really kills us at work: efficiency still trumps effectiveness. We are overworked and overburdened, all in the name of doing more, faster, and with less. Practices that lead to short-term results and shareholder value take precedence over those that lead to sustainable success. In my experience, most employees don't care about profit and shareholder value. We don't like being treated like machines. We like to be trusted to make decisions and do a good job.

Granted, there have been major shifts toward treating people as intelligent, responsible adults who want to, and can, make decisions and do a good job on their own. This approach is catching on slowly—more slowly than it should in my opinion, given the reality of the demands we face in our organizations.

It's Time to Debunk Old and Harmful Myths about Work

Outdated myths and beliefs about the nature of work and what we can expect of it are far too pervasive in spite of the obvious reasons to approach work differently in our current era. True, many of us know that it's time to debunk the myths and to claim the right to be happy and truly fulfilled at work. But when we ask for more, well-meaning friends and family tell us to check our unrealistic expectations and pull out old sayings like, "That's why they call it work." Or, when we complain about not being trusted to make decisions or being asked to do things that are counter to our values, people say, "Stop making trouble. Be grateful that you even *have* a job. Do what you're told and you'll be fine."

In the end, far too many of us accept the notion that work is not where we can be fully human, not where we can realize our potential or our dreams. We pursue goals that don't jive with our values or our own hopes for the future. We accept being treated as "doers," not people. Over time, we give in and give up and bring as little as possible of ourselves to work. We direct some of our intelligence to the task at hand but hold back our most creative ideas and our discretionary effort. We rely on our experience to do a decent job, but we resist learning and change.

Working like this is merely a way to make a living. No one likes it. Ultimately, we lose interest and hide out, or we get mad and actively disrupt or even harm our companies. Either way, we can lose sight of the best of ourselves—our values, our desire to have real impact, our hopes and dreams, and the desire to have good relationships with bosses and coworkers. We even try to shut down what makes us human.

But, organizations aren't filled with mindless automatons that live for the privilege of serving the god of profit; they never were. And as the knowledge revolution takes the world by storm, more and more of us *think* for a living, rather than *make* for a living, even in manufacturing. We need our brains to work at their best, and in order for that to happen we need physical, psychological, and spiritual well-being.

We need to replace outdated beliefs with new ways of understanding what we can expect from work—and from each other. To start with, we need to create workplaces that honor our humanity and foster common decency, camaraderie, mutual respect, and sustainable success. In order to make changes of this magnitude, each of us needs to examine how we think about work—why we do it, what we are striving for, and what drives us.

Remember, too, that while there is a kernel of truth in these myths about work, there's more wrong about them than right. Sure, work can be hard—very hard sometimes. But it is also where we learn and grow. It's where we can achieve greatness and provide deeply satisfying experiences for others. And, while we need to manage our emotions at work, we simply can't leave them at the door. Feelings matter, and they can help us tremendously.

Most of us recognize the truth and want to steer clear of the old myths that keep us stuck and unhappy at work. But to do so, we first must take responsibility for our own, often destructive, mindsets—what I call the *happiness traps*.

The Happiness Traps

Happiness traps are common and they're dangerous. But once we become aware of these traps, we can free ourselves to engage with work differently. To begin, though, we must take ownership and not allow ourselves to be trapped by stress and overwork, the desire for money, misplaced ambition, what we think we should do, or even by a sense of helplessness. Each of these five traps threatens happiness and well-being, and most of us find ourselves caught in at least one of them. Let's start with one of the most common traps: letting work take over our lives.

The Overwork Trap

Most of us work hard and we work a lot. We are often proud of how many hours we put in and how much we try to accomplish. But there's a downside. We spend every waking moment *doing* something—checking our email, talking, dashing off a text. We're always behind, running as fast as we can to catch up. We live with a great deal of stress, often to the point of burning out. We may know what we can do to make work and life better and to become happier, but there just isn't enough time to do it.

We don't have time for friends, exercise, or sleep.[5] We eat terrible food on the run. We don't have time to play with our kids, or even listen to them. Work prevents us from taking that long weekend off, and we don't stay home when we're sick. We don't take time to get to know people at work or put ourselves in their shoes before we jump to conclusions. Or we think, "Once I finish this project (or these emails or these meetings), then I'll do something that makes me feel good about myself and my work." But it never happens.

We live in a world where overwork is overvalued.[6] I see several reasons why this is happening. First, most of our organizations are chaotic and in constant flux, leaving us to deal with incessant transformation. Second, flatter, leaner organizations and ultracompetitive markets require us to do more with less. Third, globalization means we work across time zones. In practice, long days are common: early-morning and late-night conference calls are the norm; I know leaders who are expected to get up at 2 a.m. to attend video conferences. And fourth, as technology has advanced, many of us are doing tasks that others used to do—or do for us.

Then, there's the big one: that little device we carry everywhere is a demanding master. Our work is literally in our pockets—or on the nightstand. We click on texts, tweets, and email every few minutes, even during the middle of the night and, for sure, as soon as we get up in the morning. It's astounding, really, how powerful the compulsion is to connect, and much good comes of it, obviously. But as Arianna Huffington says in her book *Thrive*, "Overconnectivity is the snake in our digital Garden of Eden."[7] Even when we resist the urge, it's like a siren call, letting us know that things we have to do—or worry about—are a click away. Now, mind you, technology doesn't make us work so much; we do it to ourselves.

As *Harvard Business Review*'s Sarah Green Carmichael writes, "We log too many hours because of a mix of inner drivers, like ambition, machismo, greed, anxiety, guilt, enjoyment, pride, the pull of short-term rewards, a desire to prove we're important, or an overdeveloped sense of duty." Sometimes, too, work is an escape. When our jobs are less stressful than home, work becomes "a haven, a place to feel confident and in control."[8]

Regardless of the reason, overwork has become so prevalent that "busy" is the most common answer I get when I ask people how they are doing. I know far too many managers who log ten-plus hours a day, get on the computer or the phone first thing Saturday morning, and don't take any vacations. Or they work the entire time they are away. But just because everyone's doing this doesn't mean it supports effectiveness or happiness.[9]

Overwork is not good for us. And it's not sustainable. It leads to health problems. It compounds the stress that results from our demanding jobs and lives. It also has a negative impact on relationships. Escaping into our work doesn't solve problems in the long term at home or at work; it usually makes these problems worse.

What overwork does is to keep us stuck and striving. Working like this also shuts down our ability to decipher what we should be doing—that which will have greatest impact and move us positively toward the future. And when we are shut down like this, it's very hard to be happy.

The first step out of the overwork trap is to try to figure out why you are working so much. Is it really because you have to? Or is it a habit? Or is something deeper going on, like trying to escape your home life or prove your importance? If you can honestly face up to the reasons you are overworking, you can at least change yourself, even if the world around you remains demanding.

The Money Trap

Money is great. Until our desire for it overshadows reason.

I remember sitting with a client a few years ago, talking about her plans for retirement. She worked for a large firm in Europe—a successful company that had handsomely rewarded her and the other executives over the years. She'd planned well and had a fortune set aside for the next phase of life.

But she couldn't bring herself to leave the job, even though she had really done all she could or wanted to in the company. She told me, "I just need another couple of million in the bank before I can leave."

This sounds insane. But how many of us have stayed in jobs that we hate because the money was good? Or taken a promotion that we didn't want or weren't suited for because it came with a raise?

We all work for money, and yes, money is nice; ask anyone who doesn't have it. But some people just can't get enough. A few of them are greedy, true. But for most people, obsessing about pay raises and bank accounts isn't about greed, and it's not even really about money. There's something deeper going on: the decision to choose money over happiness is fueled by insecurity, social comparison, and the need to display one's power for all to see.

Let's take insecurity first. Wanting money to keep us alive is not about insecurity; that's rational and sane. But, like my client in the beginning of the story, a lot of people feel as if they are close to the edge of poverty and starvation when they are nowhere near either one. They are constantly afraid that, somehow, what they have will disappear and they will be in danger. This kind of insecurity often comes from having had tough experiences—like being poor—and never quite accepting that things have changed. Insecurity also comes from the belief that we aren't good enough. We suffer from the imposter syndrome and are terrified that people will find out. Money, we think, will fool them into believing we are deserving of our success.

Then there's social comparison: you see your colleagues driving nice cars, wearing beautiful clothes, and living in big, gorgeous houses. You've got a nice car, too; you dress well and have a nice home. But it eats at you: the way you see it, they have more than you do, and you feel the need to prove to them that you are an equal. So, you set out to get whatever it is that you think will make you look better, make it clear to everyone that you fit in— that you are at the top of the heap.

That's where the need for power comes in. In most parts of the world, money is linked to influence and prestige.[10] There's nothing wrong with wanting to influence one's company or society, and having power allows us to exert control over our own lives. That's a good thing. But, when the desire for power overtakes our other needs to the point that we will do anything to get or keep it, we're in deep trouble.

When we feel we *must* have money and the power that goes with it, that we must display our wealth for others to see, then we've crossed into dangerous territory. At this point, we make decisions to choose emptiness over happiness at work—just to get more cash. The money trap plays out at work all the time: you can see it in those people who are constantly obsessed with it. All the mental energy to calculate, lobby, and worry about money is siphoned away from their jobs and the people who depend on them.

Just think what work and life would be like if we could more deeply understand what really satisfies us, what really makes us happy. Wouldn't it be better if money was an outcome that followed our good work rather than a goal in itself? To get here, we have to let go of old narratives that keep us striving for more money, more power. The same goes for the next happiness trap: ambition.

The Ambition Trap

This trap is linked to something we usually think of as good: ambition. But, when our ambition is coupled with an overdeveloped focus on competition and winning, we can find ourselves in trouble.

Consider "Delphine." She's been ambitious all her life. In school, an A– left her feeling like a failure. She was highly competitive on the playing field in college, which won her friends and high praise, at first. Later on, though, her friends gave her a wide berth. Her single-minded focus on winning took the fun out of the game. And, when the team didn't win, she made people feel unworthy.

Delphine's ambition, competitiveness, and obsession for winning served her fairly well early in her career. The people above her knew she'd do just about anything to get a job done. When she was promoted, however, the dynamic of her sports days played out once again. She was a controlling, demoralizing manager. Her career plateaued early, and she had no idea why.

Delphine's story is common: some people put their own personal ambition above morals, ethics, and reason. They're blinded by their desire to win and will do just about anything to come out on top.

There's nothing inherently wrong with winning, and I know people who manage their ambition well. But winning is downright destructive when other people get hurt, when it becomes the most important goal, when you are willing to sacrifice *anything* to achieve your goal and to hell with the costs and consequences.

Early in my career, I saw this in action. I was teaching a graduate course on leadership in a college that prided itself on its smart students. They were dynamic young people from all over the world, and I enjoyed them immensely—except for one young man. He'd arrive late to class and then regale his classmates with clever (but uninformed) comments on the topic at hand. I could see how badly he wanted to appear better than them, and I spent extra time with him doing a bit of gentle coaching. He wasn't interested. He basically told me that he knew more about leadership than I ever would, thanks to his time on a professional sports team. He started skipping classes and turning in subpar work. I failed him.

He asked to meet, which I gladly did; I wanted to give him a chance to rewrite his papers and pass the course (and maybe learn something along the way). When he got to my office, however, he grabbed me by the shirt and threw me up against the wall, saying, "No one, but no one, fails me. Change the grade to an A." Needless to say, his hypercompetitive, win-lose mentality had finally gotten him into really big trouble.

I thought he'd be expelled, or worse. In the end, though, we decided to give him one more chance. Sure, I was angry, but I got over it. I saw a wounded person, not a criminal. I crafted a plan for him to reflect on his experiences as a leader in his sports teams. He went along with it, grudgingly, because the alternatives were worse. Then, when thinking about his problems on the sports teams he cared so much about, a lightbulb went on.

He came to see that his ambition was driving him to compete with *everyone*: his classmates, me, even his faraway teammates who were also pursuing degrees. He realized that the constant pursuit of the win hadn't helped him—or his teams—to be better. He also saw that it wasn't the win he was after; it was approval. By rooting out what was really driving him, he was able to find healthier ways to get what he wanted.

This young man learned a few very important lessons. First, success isn't really success when we define it as a win-lose, zero-sum game. Second, hypercompetitiveness in the workplace leaves us empty and unfulfilled, hurts our ability to lead effectively, and makes us no fun to be around. Finally, when ambition and the desire to win at all costs take over, there's usually something deeper going on—something we need to examine.

The "Should" Trap

The next happiness trap is a big one, one all of us face at some point in our careers: doing something simply because we *should*, rather than because we truly want to. This trap is pervasive because it's tied to how we learn to live in society and our organizations, too.

Society gives us rules to live by—rules we learn very early in life that guide everything we think, say, and do. These rules are often so much a part of the fabric of life that we become programmed to obey "shoulds" and "should nots," almost as if we are on autopilot. Think about the baby waving bye-bye, or children raising their hands in class. Grown-ups say "good morning" to strangers and don't wear bathing suits to work. We don't expect a sales associate to laugh at what we choose to purchase, and we don't imagine we will be punched if we are slow to step on the gas at a green light. These rules are a few of thousands we know and live by—many of which help us to interact in our families and communities.

But, some of the cultural rules that guide us at work are outdated and destructive, especially those that limit or constrain our dreams. For example, in most parts of the world, there are rules, often based on gender, about what kind of work we are supposed to do. Men, the rules tell us, must provide for their families and "help out" a bit at home, while women should do the all-encompassing task of family management: virtually all of the housework, cooking, caring for children, managing finances, and planning and orchestrating the family's daily activities.

This rule simply doesn't work when at least half of the paid workforce is female. Many men and women don't adhere to this particular "should" anymore. But, as almost any man who has had to tell his boss he can't come in because he's caring for a sick child knows, society's norms have an impact on the workplace, too, and there are penalties for not following them.

Organizations, too, have rules we follow. These "shoulds" and "should nots" are part of company culture and they govern everything from attire to attitudes to who can take certain jobs—and who cannot.

"Shoulds" in the Workplace

Some years ago, I was teaching two executive leadership programs during the same week, in the same building. One group was from Wall Street, one from the high-tech industry. To illustrate organizational culture, we'd asked them if they could decipher beliefs, values, and ways of doing business simply by looking at one another.

We asked the members of the two classes to stand facing each other across a room and to call out what they noticed. They quickly pointed out obvious differences in clothing, shoes, even haircuts and personal grooming. Then came the surprise: these savvy, sophisticated executives started cracking rude jokes about the "losers" on the other side of the room. For instance, the Wall Street group members ridiculed the others' more casual dress and jeered about laziness. In return, members of the tech company laughed at their counterparts' expensive clothes. Words like "egghead," "arrogant," and "empty suit" flew out of people's mouths. We were stunned.

The experience revealed a lot about the unspoken rules that guide work and life. To be successful in these companies, we discovered, people had to obey the "shoulds" about how to dress, how to talk, and how to manage time. There were also unspoken rules about who could be hired and promoted, and who should lead. If, for example, an interviewee showed up with even slightly scuffed shoes to the Wall Street interview, he was automatically disqualified. And in both companies, to be a senior manager, you had to be married. Not much shocks me anymore, but this surely did.

On the positive side, conforming to certain workplace norms helps us understand one another; in essence, "shoulds" give us a shared language. This is great when it comes to rules that help us work well together, like respect, timeliness, or polite, friendly conversations at the beginning of a meeting. The problem is, however, that too many of our workplace rules don't serve us well. Who cares, really, whether someone wears short or long sleeves to work? Or high heels or flats? Do scuffed shoes affect intelligence? And does marital status affect one's ability to lead? Of course not.

Workplace "shoulds" are such powerful drivers of our beliefs and behaviors that we often go along with rules that make no sense. We even compromise our personal wishes and values in order to fit in. This can be fine, but conformity doesn't usually support original, creative contributions at work.[11] And, for many of us, the "shoulds" we are forced to adhere to—whether they are society's or our organizations'—are truly at odds with who we are and what we believe. That is soul destroying. When it gets to this point, we're trapped.

"Shoulds" Can Trap Our Dreams

When trying to understand how "shoulds" affect us, we need to examine more than just the day-to-day rules. We need to look at the "big" rules: those that guide us in the larger choices we make about life and work. Once again, some norms actually help us, like those that guide us to complete our education or learn a trade. Following this rule prepares us to help our families, contribute to society, and be an important member of an organization. But, some of these same rules drive us toward goals we don't want to achieve and work we don't enjoy.

"Shoulds" can even push us into the wrong job. Oprah Winfrey, for example, landed a plum job as an anchor in Baltimore very early in her career. This job was perfect, she thought, exactly what she should do if she wanted to pursue her dreams of becoming a successful television journalist. Apparently, though, she cared too much about the stories and the people she reported on, and this didn't fit with the network's image of how a news anchor should behave. Oprah left that job and took another on a struggling talk show. On this new show, she felt she was where she belonged— where she could use all of her talent and truly enjoy her work.[12]

Or, take Jennifer Duvalier, an executive I've worked with who has excelled in her career from her very first job as a banker.[13] Just out of college, Jennifer landed a great role with a prestigious financial services institution. It was exactly the kind of job that she thought she *should* take to launch her career. However, she soon noticed that it wasn't what she'd expected. Sure, it was challenging and fast paced. But everything and everyone was constrained by bureaucracy and unspoken rules about things like who could talk to whom in the hierarchy or who was allowed to have a new idea (not the young recruits, that's for sure). Jennifer wasn't happy. She couldn't even begin to bring the best of herself to this job—the "shoulds" and "should nots" wouldn't let her.

She told me about a particular moment when she was working in Paris. "Sitting there as the meeting went on around me, I remember thinking, 'I don't find this in any way interesting. I'm not really learning anything. It's of no value to me, and it's clear they don't want my contributions.' I was feeling completely disconnected, and not in any way engaged or stimulated."

Jennifer then realized that good job or not, she couldn't stay just because she was supposed to, just because it was the kind of job her friends envied. The job just didn't provide her what she wanted in her work: excitement, adventure, learning, and the chance to make a difference.

She quit. Soon thereafter, Jennifer was hired by a global company and was quickly entrusted with coaching senior executives to become better leaders. There's nothing notable about this except that at the time, Jennifer was less than a decade out of college. How could she possibly reach these smart, seasoned, wily executives? She did it. And the reason she could was that she was wise beyond her years. She'd faced up to the "should" trap and was able to help these leaders free themselves from old habits and patterns that kept them from being their best.

Social rules and "shoulds" are a fact of life. It's not about getting rid of them; it's about sorting through them and making conscious choices about which to follow—those that enable you to live your values, reach your potential, and be happy.

You may see yourself in one of these four traps—or even all of them. And you may do quite a lot to avoid these traps. If you do, you likely believe in your capacity to influence yourself and the world around you. This belief that we can make things happen is critical to happiness. Without it, you fall into the last trap: helplessness.

The Helplessness Trap

Some people truly believe that no matter how hard they try, they can't influence the world around them, change things, or get what they want. These are the fatalists in our midst. Chances are you don't see life this way. But this trap is becoming a lot more common as the world changes at an ever-faster pace and our organizations become more hectic and often more unpleasant places to work. As a result, many people feel that they have little or no control over what happens to them.

The helplessness trap may be the deadliest of all. It kills hope, shatters dreams, and leaves us at the mercy of others and the vagaries of our organizations. Let's look at my friend "Neal," a high-potential young manager in an engineering company, to see the impact of this dangerous trap.

When I met Neal, he was flying high on success and extremely busy; he traveled all the time, worked a lot, and had a young family. He felt like the master of his own fate. He was in charge and pushing forward at his own pace.

A few years later, I ran into Neal and was shocked at the change in him. He'd gotten a significant promotion and the money was great, but he seemed dejected, not elated as I'd have expected him to be. He explained that his job bored him to tears and he no longer saw the lifestyle as glamorous. He absolutely despised traveling and dreaded going to yet another airport and sleeping in yet another five-star hotel.

Then he told me a story that broke my heart.

"My daughter came back from summer camp last month," he began. "She's fourteen now, and for the first time in a while, I really noticed how much she's changed. Somehow I've had this image of my little girl in my head. Well, she's gone and there's this young woman in her place! And it hit me: she'll be leaving home in less than four years.

"I vowed then and there to spend more time with her.

"So, I've been trying to do things with her. I've asked her to go to the movies and I go to her soccer games. I even promised her a shopping trip with her friends. She just kept saying she was busy, or ignored me. I thought 'Teenagers!' But then last week, when I picked her up from a game and asked her to do something with me, she said, 'Dad, if you think you can disappear for my entire childhood and then just show up and be my best friend, you're wrong.'"

This was a major wake-up call for Neal. But, he told me, he had no idea what to do. He felt totally trapped and helpless. He didn't believe for a minute that he could rebuild the relationship with his daughter. He thought he'd ruined it for good.

As we talked, it became clear that he felt trapped at work, too. He tried to justify his choice to take the new job, telling himself the money was enough. It wasn't, of course, and as the industry continued to change, those big bonuses dried up just as leadership began putting more and more pressure on him to cut costs, deliver more revenue, and speed up.

Neal felt that he had no control whatsoever, at work or at home. He couldn't do what he felt was right for his employees and he couldn't quit, either. He told his wife, "It's a treadmill and there's no way I can get off." She countered, saying, "You can get off anytime you want." She went on to tell him that he could also fix his relationship with his daughter. Neal didn't see it this way at all. He had completely stopped believing that he could do anything to improve his situation at work—or at home. Fatalism like this kills hope and limits our lives—something I learned, too.

Many years ago, I lived a very different life. Some of it was great: I was a young mom, passionately engaged with my kids. I was also poor and working menial jobs. I did everything I could to find meaning in the work, and for a time, I succeeded. But after a while, I became discouraged. I knew I could do more, but I'd been stuck for so long in a cycle of poverty that I had no idea how to get out. The very idea of waitressing and cleaning other people's houses for the rest of my life made me want to cry—and give up. But I didn't. It took a lot of courage, some really good friends, and a lot of soul searching to help me break that cycle.

Maybe you have been—or are currently—in a situation where you felt hopeless and trapped, as I did, or maybe you're staying at a company because you are afraid to change jobs. Perhaps you feel that you will never find a job that pays as well, or you don't think any company will let you pursue your passion. Maybe you think you are too old to look for work that fulfills you. I've often heard this sort of thing from people who desperately want more from their work: more excitement, more challenge, more happiness. But they think that they "can't afford" to or they will have to "start at the bottom."

My story—and Neal's—shows that we *can* make those hard changes. The first step is the hardest; it takes blind faith and courage to take action when we believe we are unable to influence our world. Neal began, slowly, to take some control back, starting with an unplanned trip with his family—an adventure vacation that he knew his daughter would love. To his surprise, this step had an added benefit: despite his fears, no one at work had a problem with him taking extra time off.

Activate Your Emotional Intelligence

Almost everyone falls prey to old myths and happiness traps that keep us down and prevent us from creating or sustaining the work life we want. In this exercise, you will look at how and why you've adopted certain myths and happiness traps. Reflecting on your beliefs will help you to hone your self-awareness—a competency that is essential if you are to break free from mindsets that no longer serve you well.

1. Review the common myths and the happiness traps I've discussed in this chapter. Choose one or two that you know affect you and impact your work.

2. Now, let's look at where this happiness trap or myth came from. Draw a timeline from your birth year until today, and write notes about major childhood, school, work, and life events.

3. Next, on your timeline, note when in your life you first started adopting this myth or happiness trap. Where or from whom did you get messages that you had to think or behave this way? How did you feel about these messages and what was the impact on you?

4. Next, on your timeline, note when this myth or trap has affected your choices and outcomes. Jot some thoughts about how it has actually helped you at times, as well as when it has interfered with your happiness. Consider this question in terms of physical health, emotional well-being, and work.

5. What concrete actions can you take today, next week, and next month to leverage the positive aspects of the myth or trap and minimize the negative?

He took this as a win and pushed back in other areas where he'd not felt he had much control, such as fighting for what his employees needed to do their jobs. Here, too, he made progress. Over the next year, he took ever-bolder steps to reconstruct his family life as well as his work life. It's working. The Neal I knew years ago is back.

Old myths and happiness traps can keep us stuck. But it doesn't have to be that way. You can do things to change how you think about your work. It starts with claiming your power, as Neal and I did. Then, it takes hard work. But it's worth it.

Breaking Free

The first step toward happiness is to break free of the myths I talked about at the beginning of the chapter. You are not a machine and your company doesn't own you for forty—or sixty, or eighty—hours each week. Your ideas, needs, and desires matter. So does your happiness. Here's the best part: if you fight to crush these old-fashioned myths about the painful nature of work, both you and your organization will be more successful.

To truly break free, though, we have to do more. We have to delve deeply into the mindsets and the actions that go with them that keep us from being happy at work. Why, we need to ask ourselves, do we work all the time? Why are we so seduced by money and power? Is our ambition and desire to win serving us or hurting us? Why are we so trapped by what we feel we should do rather than pursuing what we want to do? And why do we sometimes give up on being happy at all? To answer these questions, we need to return to emotional intelligence.

The Antidote to the Happiness Traps: Emotional Intelligence

If we are to combat these outdated myths and the happiness traps and take control of our own happiness, we need to look at how we think about work, how we feel about our choices, and what we do day-to-day. For this, we need more than a modicum of emotional intelligence.[14]

Emotional intelligence is the capacity to understand one's own and others' emotions and to deal with them in a way that leads

FIGURE 2-1

Emotional intelligence competencies

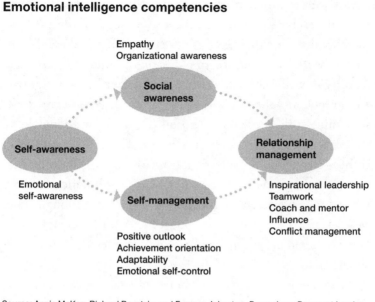

Source: Annie McKee, Richard Boyatzis, and Frances Johnston, *Becoming a Resonant Leader* (Boston: Harvard Business Press, 2008), 25.

to resonance in relationships as well as individual and collective success. There are twelve emotional intelligence competencies, as you can see in figure 2-1. These competencies help us to be effective at work. They also help us to avoid and break free from the happiness traps.

Self-Awareness

Avoiding the happiness traps starts with emotional self-awareness. You must tune in to those faint whispers in your mind, those almost imperceptible feelings of "something's not right."

Learning to notice and understand your feelings is a first step toward understanding what drives you—good and bad. That discomfort you feel when you buck a cultural rule or a "should" at work, for example, might be a sign that you're actually afraid of being excluded, of not fitting in. Going a bit deeper, you might realize that this fear has little or nothing to do with your current work situation; it's an old habit of mind that no longer serves you well. The same might go for that intense urge you feel to look at your email at 8 p.m. Is the urge rational? Does something truly need your attention? Or is it an irrational desire to work all the time so no one finds out you aren't on top of things—that you are suffering from the imposter syndrome? Maybe, as you practice self-awareness, you will notice that you are feeling a bit down, a bit helpless, in the face of tough times at work. This knowledge—if you catch it early enough—can help you avoid becoming fatalistic and powerless to change your situation.

These are just examples, of course, of what we can find if we listen to our feelings, track our moods, and work to understand what they are telling us. By doing this personal work, we are preparing ourselves to recognize why we get trapped and taking a step toward action.

Self-Management

The happiness traps I've written about in this chapter are common and *powerful*. That's why you need emotional self-control. Emotional self-control helps us stay tuned in to our feelings, even when we don't like what we discover. If, for example, we find we are trapped by "shoulds" and rules at work, we are likely to feel frightened when thinking about doing something different. That's because we've been indoctrinated. We follow societal and organizational rules without even noticing them. They just *are*. It takes effort to ask hard questions about whether or not particular rules are valid—for us or our organizations. It takes even more effort to change long-held habits that go along with "shoulds" and "should nots."

So when you realize that looking at your email at night is coming from a personal insecurity, you're not going to feel particularly good. Emotional self-control enables you to manage these kinds of feelings so they don't get the better of you. Moreover, you can then actively choose to see things differently—to adapt and shift your mindset from negative to a more positive way of viewing yourself and your situation. Managing your feelings like this enables you to bravely take action, rather than remain frozen in place.

Once you know what's driving you, self-management helps you shift your attention. This subtle but powerful internal change supports willpower, focus, and courage—all of which you need to do the hard work of breaking free.[15]

Social Awareness and Relationship Management

Honing your ability to understand others, groups, and organizations also helps you deal with old-fashioned beliefs about work and happiness traps. When you focus on empathizing with people and understanding your organizational environment, you can see what is coming from inside you, and what's coming from others or your company.

With this knowledge, you are better equipped to make choices about what you will or will not accept at work. For example, you may recognize that everyone in your organization is overworking—reading and sending emails at all hours, skipping lunch and weekends, driving each other crazy. This knowledge helps you see that you are actually under pressure to conform—that it's not your insecurity driving this behavior. With this knowledge, you are more likely to choose actions that enable you to break free from the trap of working all the time. There might be an added benefit, too, as you begin to create a microculture on your team where overworking is not overvalued. The same goes for other traps that people often share in a workplace. Once you see that they are part of the culture, you can do something about them—at least in your immediate circle.

The most important lesson about happiness traps is that you can always do something to free yourself or at least mitigate the impact on you and others. It's not always easy, and you might have to work hard, so guard against discouragement.

Don't give up. Happiness matters. Positive emotions like enthusiasm, hope, and excitement provide the energy to sustain the inevitable hard knocks we all experience along the way. And, when we are happy at work, others "catch" our feelings and are inspired to find happiness, too.[16]

Personal Reflection and Mindful Practice

In these exercises you will gain insight about how you view work and plan for how to let go of mindsets that don't work for you—the myths and traps that make you unhappy. With this knowledge, you can prepare yourself to craft a work life that truly fulfills you.

Breaking Free from Traps and Destructive Mindsets

1. Which of the happiness traps keep me in my comfort zone? Which traps actually make me feel safe? Which

traps, if I'm honest with myself, are excuses for not taking the risk to pursue what I really want?

2. Which of the happiness traps keep me from pursuing my dreams for a better job, a great career, or real fulfillment in the job I have now?

3. Which happiness traps do I keep others in? How does this serve me and them positively? How does it hurt me and them?

An Exercise in Self-Awareness, Self-Management, and Courage

It isn't always easy to look at mindsets we've adopted that keep us trapped, and may even affect others negatively, too. But, courageously looking at happiness traps provides a foundation for taking control—for managing ourselves as we take steps to change how we think about work. This exercise will support you in this journey.

1. Choose the happiness trap that most affects you.

2. How is this happiness trap helping or hurting you?

3. Next, consider your relationships and how this happiness trap affects them. Other people often benefit (or think they do) when we are trapped. Or, they can get hurt. Who in your life benefits from the happiness trap you are in? Who is harmed? To illustrate, draw some circles and put the names of important people in each one (your boss, people who influence you at work, mentors, loved ones). Now, in each circle, jot some notes about how each person or team is affected by you being trapped.

4. Now, imagine a life without the happiness trap you've been writing about. What would this freedom feel like? What would you do? What benefits would others experience if you were to free yourself? To bring this to life, write three paragraphs as if you are already in the future, starting with, "It is now three years since I broke free. I feel . . . I am now . . . The people in my life are . . ."

CHAPTER 3

The Power of Purpose

*Live Your Values and
Make a Difference*

A few years ago, my husband and I were working in Cambodia. With the help of the United Nations, our team had developed a program to teach people how to lead in their communities as a means of combating HIV and AIDS.[1] Our participants came from all walks of life: they were monks, government ministers, community organizers, scholars, and ordinary citizens. Some had been part of the Pol Pot regime. Virtually all of them had lost loved ones during the genocide. Trust between and among individual people and the groups they represented was low or nonexistent.

Together with our team and our Cambodian colleagues, we tried to find something that would unite people, something that would help them build solid relationships as they took on the growing threat of HIV and AIDS in their country. It was a struggle. How could survivors and former soldiers ever find common ground?

We discovered the answer when we visited the magnificent temples of Angkor Wat near the city of Siem Reap. While we were there, we saw evidence of an inspired ancient people—a culture that was rich in intellectual and artistic achievements and awe-inspiring tributes to their spiritual beliefs. We were shepherded through the sacred sites by a brilliant and knowledgeable guide, a man who took great pride in his work.

Our guide was excited about his country's future, and he felt that he had an important role to play in the burgeoning tourist trade. He was well suited to the job: he spoke at least three languages fluently and knew his country's history from ancient times to today. He was steeped in global economics and understood the sociopolitical dynamics of the region and the world. I was stunned to find out that he hadn't been educated overseas and had not attended a world-renowned university. He'd never left the Siem Reap region of Cambodia, and he'd never attended school. He didn't even have a childhood: he had been a boy soldier, forced to fight after his parents, grandparents, uncles, and aunts had been killed.

We talked about what kept him going during those years and how he had turned his passion for his country and its people into a fulfilling career. He told us about the many visitors he'd guided through the temples, how much their interest in his country meant to him, and how much he valued the opportunity to learn about his guests and their faraway homes. He spoke of being deeply happy with his young family and his work. Over the next few days, he told us the story of how he'd survived and found his way to a purposeful, meaningful, and joyous life in spite of a situation most of us can't even imagine.

When he was very young, his entire family except for one aunt was killed, most of them in front of his eyes. Then he was forced to live with the killers. As a child soldier, he saw some of the worst of humanity in his young guards and captors. But, as time went on, it became clear to him that almost all of them—young boys and teenagers alike—had had their lives stolen from them. They were all just children like he was. They were all sad.

As the youngsters began to form bonds, they did what children do—they explored, they learned, and they tried to have fun. They played at the Angkor Wat temples, which were almost completely overgrown at the time. But the children discovered beautiful statues and mysterious inscriptions that clearly *meant* something.

As a boy, our guide told us, he escaped the horror of his situation by imagining what the statues had signified—what they meant to his ancestors. He studied how some of the windows captured the sun's rays in a way that was obviously intentional. Over time, he began to decipher some of the inscriptions on the temples. He realized he needed to learn to read his modern language so he could study history, and he found older boys willing to teach him. He also asked the few remaining adults around him what they knew about the temples and the inscriptions. Slowly, he started to create a picture in his mind of the ancient world and the Cambodian people of long ago.

He was fascinated by what drove his ancestors to build these incredible structures, what motivated them, and what they sought to achieve. Clearly, they were a brilliant and noble people. Surely they found great joy in the impossibly intricate architecture, the art they created. Maybe, he thought, their lives were hard and they searched for a better life, just as he did. His quest for knowledge gave him something to believe in, something to long for— and something meaningful to *do*.

In spite of the agony of the Pol Pot years, the boy developed tremendous insight into ancient Cambodia, along with a deep and abiding pride in his ancestors' values and beliefs. Later, as his country broke free from the bonds of dictatorship, he came to see that the powerful purpose that had saved him as a child could be the foundation for work—work that would be tied to something he cared deeply about. He also realized that he was one of the few remaining people who might be able to help the world see a different side of Cambodia. When tourists began arriving in his country, he became a student of languages, global politics, and social change. Soon he was fluent in French, English, and Russian. He could hold his own with anyone on topics as varied as history, religion, and social upheaval.

This young man was helping his nation, and he knew it. He had been called to share his country's history, and by doing so, he was living his values and making a difference. He definitely had an impact on us and our work in Cambodia. In his story, we found inspiration as well as an answer to the thorny problem of how to unite our group of diverse leaders. We discovered that many Cambodians—especially the youth—knew little about the country's impressive history. We also discovered that people were hungry to connect with their glorious past and in doing so could begin building bridges across the chasms that existed in the modern day. As our program participants came to Angkor Wat and explored their country again, they found hope in the knowledge that the people of Cambodia were once great and united, and would be again.

Our guide showed me how purpose and work go hand in hand, which is what this chapter is about. Through other stories and my own experiences, I will talk about how we can experience work as a calling, not just a job. When work is an expression of our values and we have positive impact on something we care about, we are motivated from within; we don't need others to push us or beg us to do our jobs, and we can withstand challenge and turmoil. At the end of the chapter, I will share some concrete and practical ways to find meaning in your work.

Finding Meaning in Our Work:
It's What People *Do*

Philosophers, storytellers, priests, and poets give voice to our life-long quest to find purpose in our everyday activities—at home and at work.[2] Looking back through history, there's no reason to believe that our ancestors sought meaning in stories and spiritual practices only to turn it off when they hunted or foraged or planted those first grains of wheat. Myths and prayers elevated routine tasks to the realm of the sacred. Hunting and harvesting, child rearing and cooking—all necessary for the tribe's survival, and all done in ways that expressed the tribe's most cherished beliefs and values, too.

Today, our organizations are our tribes. Work is still where we express ourselves and make a difference. But, in our hyper-industrialized world, work and life are no longer seen as vitally intertwined. Rather, we see our jobs as a means to an end, a way to earn money so we can have meaningful lives *outside* of work.

This kind of compartmentalization of work and "real" life seems reasonable on the surface, especially if we believe those old myths about work being an ugly, painful necessity. Certainly this belief is prevalent in our companies. The result, as management scholars Jeffrey Pfeffer and Robert Sutton tell us, is that "many companies do not worry that much about providing meaning and fulfillment to their people. Work is, after all, a four-letter word."[3]

But it's impossible to pull life and work apart. We are meaning-making creatures, no matter if we're sitting in an office, giving tours of historical places, hiking Mount Kilimanjaro, or eating dinner with our family. We don't give up the essential human need to do something worthwhile when we start our workday. We want to know that we're doing something that *matters*.[4]

Seeing our work as an expression of cherished values and as a way to make a contribution is the foundation of well-being, happiness, and our ongoing success. Passion for a cause fuels energy, intelligence, and creativity. And, when we see that the results of our labor will benefit ourselves and others, we want to "fight the good fight" together.

This is in part because of brain chemistry: the positive emotions that accompany purposeful, meaningful engagement in our activities enable us to be smarter, more innovative, and more adaptable. In this state, we're excited to take on new challenges and are more resilient and motivated.[5]

I have been fortunate to feel this way about my work, even when my job wasn't one that other people envied. For many years, I cleaned people's houses and waited tables. It was physical labor that didn't pay well, but I found ways to link my work to what I cared about. For instance, I once lived with an elderly woman who was caring for her ailing husband. At first, I was thrilled; I desperately needed a job. But I was also embarrassed; I had higher hopes for myself and hadn't thought I would have to do this kind of work.

Soon, though, I came to love my job in large part because I liked my employer. Plus, the house was on a cliff overlooking the ocean. The work was far from glamorous, but it included things that mattered to me: a good relationship, fun and laughter, and access to the beauty of the natural world. Over time, I found more. I realized that my skills as a companion and caregiver made a difference in these people's lives. This was deeply gratifying. I felt fulfilled and empowered. The feeling that I was doing something worthwhile and having a positive impact gave me the confidence and courage to look beyond that job. I began asking, "What else could I do to make a difference in people's lives? What do I need to do to get there?" Those questions eventually led me to my calling.

Is Your Work a Job, a Career, or a Calling?

Years later, I was able to make sense of my experience through the writings of Yale professor Amy Wrzesniewski. She and her colleagues have studied people in a variety of professions and found that we experience work in one of these three ways: a job, a career, or a calling.[6]

Work as a Job

When we see our work as (just) a job, we're focused on what we get for our labor—a paycheck and other tangible benefits like insurance. These extrinsic rewards are the reason we get up every day and go to work. Of course, there's nothing inherently wrong with simply exchanging work for money. Sometimes we just need a job to pay our bills or provide for our families.

Through my personal experience and that of my clients, however, I know that seeing work as just a job can be soul-destroying. We punch the clock, calculate how many sick days we can get away with, and dream of winning the lottery. We tell ourselves that the money's worth it, but we feel empty. When we are unable to see the impact of our work or find meaning in what we do, we often become dissatisfied and resentful. I've seen this happen to people in service jobs like housekeeping and landscaping and to high-powered, well-paid executives. Despite the vast difference in the amount of money they made, they were all equally unhappy.

Work as a Career

We might, instead, see our work as a career. Our job is then linked to a bigger picture, often advancement in a profession or a company. We see our current role as an important step toward a destination. For example, we may see ourselves having significant impact on a field or rising in an organization we care about. This can be fun and exciting and can fulfill the need for a guiding purpose at work, presumably because our career is linked to our values. This can and often does make us happy.

However, people who view work as a career are often largely motivated by things like prestige or upward mobility—things that, like money, come from outside of us. There's nothing wrong with looking forward to the next promotion or pay raise, but a singular focus on external recognition and rewards can make day-to-day work feel like a means to an end. We can find ourselves constantly seeking the next goal or prize, but each time we get that job, bonus, or raise, our ambition kicks in and we turn our attention to the next win. This isn't satisfying, as over time it feels as if we are on an eternal search for the holy grail. It gets tiring and ultimately less and less fulfilling.

I saw this happen to a manager who described himself as a "marketeer." Early on in his career, he was on fire: he learned a lot, took risks, and got the rewards he sought. Building his portfolio of experiences and jobs was his raison d'être, and he progressed just as he intended. By the time I met him, he'd held virtually every job in the marketing department and was now a senior manager. But he wasn't happy. As he put it, "I'm not hungry anymore." The progression up the ladder just didn't satisfy him as it once had, and the rewards felt empty. After a brief moment of elation at getting yet another promotion, raise, or bonus, he questioned why he was sacrificing so much for his work.

When we view our work as a career, we should ask ourselves, "To what end?" If the answer is only to advance or progress, something vital is probably missing. What that "marketeer" wanted—and what I wanted all those years ago—was to feel that work was a true calling.

Work as a Calling

When we experience our work as a calling, our efforts are not simply the means to an end, and we're not just jumping from one goal to the next. Instead, what we do every single day brings deep satisfaction. Even simple activities are seen as important, fulfilling, and meaningful.

When work is a calling, our passion motivates us from the inside out. We want to do our best because what we are doing is inherently meaningful: we find ways to express our values through our work, and we revel in the opportunity to make a difference to the people around us, our companies, and our communities. And, even when dealing with big responsibilities and the sometimes outrageous pressures that are so common in our workplaces, we're able to stay grounded and see the big picture. It's not that we don't mind—we do, and we have to take care of ourselves—but it feels worth it.

Having a calling at work is not reserved for people who have "noble" jobs like doctors, clergy, or philanthropists. Surprisingly, I've met people who work in the noblest professions and organizations in the world who see their work simply as a job or a career. And it's not uncommon for people who have all sorts of jobs—plumbers, factory workers, waiters, and grocery store clerks—to see their work as a calling. That's because it's not the job that determines whether we see it as a calling or not; it's *us*. How we view our work and how we engage with people and our tasks is what makes the difference.

This is what Amy Wrzesniewski found in her studies of janitors in hospitals. This is a tough job and not one many people would aspire to. Yet, when Wrzesniewski studied how they felt about their work, a surprising number of the janitors described their work as a career or a calling—not just a dreary job. Many saw their work as truly noble: they were helping sick people get better and healthy people stay that way by keeping the hospital clean. They saw their work as highly skilled and worthy of efforts beyond what the job demanded. For example, some would make an extra effort to learn which chemicals were least likely to create problems for certain patients. Others went even further; they acted on values like compassion and went out of their way to bring warmth and comfort to ailing, frightened patients.[7]

I've known people who serve food in cafeterias, work as compliance officers in corporations, and labor as prison guards. All of these jobs are difficult, and it would be easy to just show up and do the minimum. But the food server sees herself as the person who provides that one good meal to young students. The compliance officer sees himself as providing guidance and rules that enable people to work effectively without fear of violating ethical codes or laws. And the prison guard sees herself as a friend to lonely people.

Or take Colin Browne, a carpenter and general contractor I have known for years. Carpentry is hard work. It can, I imagine, be tiresome. Colin doesn't see it that way at all, even after thirty years on the job. He sees his work as the creation of art. Each cabinet he builds, each addition to a home, each new kitchen is made with gorgeous and sustainable natural materials. He works to ensure that he adds to the beauty of a home and that each newly constructed piece is a beautiful expression of the owner's personality.[8]

You may be wondering how to transform your job or your career into a calling. That's where "job crafting" comes in.[9] While I didn't know it at the time, this is what I did when I cared for the elderly couple in that house overlooking the ocean, how I discovered that helping people was something I lived for—not just something I did for a paycheck.

Here's how it works: first, you've got to think about work differently, change your perception about what you do and how you do it. For me, this meant thinking about my work with the elderly couple as making their lives better, rather than as washing their clothes and cleaning their bathrooms. Then you need to focus on what you do (the tasks) and whom you do it with (relationships). Both of these, with some effort, can be reframed and reformed to provide a deeper sense of meaning. For me, the first part was easy: I liked this couple, and in particular, I loved spending time with the woman. She had a lot of wisdom and frankly taught me a lot about being a grown-up. Reforming the tasks wasn't quite as easy, but I found ways to do more things outside so I could take in that ocean view. I also became a creative cook. I was inspired and excited about cooking healthy meals that tasted great. This was meaningful and fun, too.

Over the years, I have applied these lessons to each job I've had, and I've been able to find meaning in the work I've done in organizations of all sorts. Along the way, I've encountered people who have taught me even more about how to stay connected with meaning and purpose, even when our jobs are challenging. It's become increasingly clear to me that if we are to experience our work as a calling, we've got to understand *which values matter to us* and then *act on these values to have positive impact.*

The Courage to Lead from Your Values

Dun & Bradstreet is a financial services company that has transformed itself time and again over the two centuries it has been in business. Change is a constant at D&B, both because of technological innovation and because clients understand more, want more, and don't accept the traditional notion that financial services should be performed in secret by experts. Therefore, D&B's business processes as well as its culture must evolve constantly.

In an attempt to keep up with continuous change, some leaders focus so intensely on business objectives that they bulldoze through people, crushing everything in their path. Not Josh Peirez, chief operating officer and president. He is committed to leading in a way that is consistent with his core belief that everyone deserves respect, no matter the circumstance.[10]

All of this played out when the company's ambitious strategy called for yet another business transformation, one that required radical changes to how people did their jobs. Josh was under pressure to move fast. But, rather than shifting into execution mode, he decided to invest time in understanding what people—wherever they sat in the organization—found fulfilling in their current ways of working and what got in their way. Josh said, "I hoped to understand the values that drive our team members, what inspired them, and what I could do to amplify this. The more time I spent talking and listening to them about those elements rather than just about business issues, the more appreciation I had for their perspectives and the more ideas I had about how I could help. If you give people space, they'll find the solutions themselves. They'll understand how what they do every day has some purpose: to help the company, the customer, and society." Josh knew that motivating people to change with the evolving business necessitated preserving what people found most meaningful in their jobs and connecting it to a broader purpose. His role was to create space for people to identify that purpose for themselves, to help them feel heard, and to remove any obstacles that got in the way.

This may sound like common sense, but frankly, in my experience, very few managers do this as well as they might. This is often because of a perceived lack of time or pressure from above to move fast. Some managers pay lip service to the idea that "everyone has a voice," but they don't create environments in which people dare to talk about what really matters, or they ignore viewpoints that aren't convenient.

Josh, though, strives to build the kinds of relationships where people feel empowered and comfortable speaking candidly. Team members talked with Josh about roadblocks and aspects of their work that made their jobs challenging, things like processes and policies that needed to be refreshed so D&B could move even faster. This struck a chord for Josh because it flew in the face of another one of his core values: "It's tough for me to see bureaucracy get in the way of achieving outcomes. I want a fast-paced, fast-moving, decisive, highly autonomous culture and a work environment that's incredibly productive as a result. From my own personal experience, when there's a policy that is unnecessarily restrictive and causes work-arounds, the intention of the policy is suboptimized and can significantly hamper both the productivity and the morale of the company. I care about the people I work with, and cannot stand to see them challenged by unnecessary policies and processes. As a leader, my voice is important in ensuring that our policies and processes do what they are intended to do in the most effective ways possible. I couple this with my belief in listening to team members and enabling them to find and implement solutions that will most effectively achieve our company's purpose."

Josh acted on his values to create a clear path for change—one that allowed people to do more of what they loved. He essentially did job crafting on an organizational level. For example, he broke down traditional lines of communication so anyone, anywhere, who needed senior management help with a client could get it with a simple phone call. He also did a few things that seemed symbolic but were expressions of his core values. He became a champion for policies such as unlimited sick time and a more relaxed dress code that allowed people to wear clothes that were suitable to the work they were doing on a given day. His commitment to respect and compassion as fundamental human rights helped people see him as someone with integrity, someone willing to always do the right thing for the people—honoring their identity and talents.

It wasn't all fun, of course. The journey of a business transformation is arduous. Josh was putting in long hours and the work was intense. Understandably, team members struggled with ongoing change: there was little respite and the pressures multiplied. Josh knew that everyone was working hard but he felt that despite everyone's efforts things weren't moving fast enough. He found himself a bit more on guard than usual, which was unlike him. He began to wonder if the teams were growing weary and uninspired and he also sensed that people might be holding back their thoughts and frustrations from him.

As he reflected on the team's hard work and the situation, Josh realized that he had become a bit less focused on team members' concerns and worries. So, he quickly shifted his mindset to place his values front and center. First, he reemphasized his belief in the importance of valuing people—which to Josh means respecting them, caring about them, and seeking to understand their perspectives. He also recommitted to creating an environment where work processes were simple and straightforward. And, as he put it, "Another core value is the belief in the fundamental goodness of people." Josh explained to me, "I believe that people are inherently trustworthy, and that has shaped my view of everything I do at work." By reconnecting to these core values, Josh was able to ensure that the relationships he had with his team members were fortified. The level of candor increased and remained high, and people felt that their ideas were heard and that they mattered. Even amidst this challenging time, Josh's leaders and team members remained inspired by him. They also remained dedicated to their collective successes and empowered to further transform the company.

By focusing on his values, Josh excelled at his job as a leader. He was resilient when business challenges emerged and he remained deeply motivated to lead and support his team members to achieve their aims. This is what purpose does for us at work: it drives us toward what we value.

Activate Your Emotional Intelligence

We spend a lot of time and energy at work trying to understand our strengths and weaknesses so we can perform better and be successful. As important as this is, it pales in comparison to understanding our values. This knowledge, I believe, is the most important aspect of self-awareness when it comes to being happier at work.

1. List five values that define who you are (hint: one way to tell is to imagine if it was taken away from you or if you were forbidden to believe as you do or live according to this value). Now, list five more for a total of ten core values. Circle those that have led you to the work you do today.

2. For each of the values that led you to your job or career, write some notes about how you can express this value so your work feels more like a calling and less like "just a job" or a career.

3. Now, reflect on and write some notes about which aspects of your work align with your view of your purpose in life. Remember, it's not always the big things (e.g., "I work for the United Nations in support of human rights"). More often it's the small, ordinary things like "Every day I can find ways to help people learn and grow."

Purpose: Motivation from Within

Motivation that comes from inside us is a far more potent force than any carrot or stick used by our boss or the company. This flies in the face of what we've been taught—that if our manager offers us more money, better assignments, a promotion, we will do what we are told and perform at our best. This couldn't be further from the truth. Studies show that people actually become less interested in tasks when they are externally rewarded.[11] It's true—try rewarding a child for what he likes to do. Over time, that child will lose interest in things he once loved and only do it to get "paid."[12]

Real rewards, the kind that help us sustain commitment, engagement, and happiness, come from within us.[13] That's why purpose is such a powerful motivator. The deep and abiding belief that what we do has meaning is the kind of internal driver that makes everything we do feel worthwhile. And, like Josh and the people who work for him, we also want to have control over *how* we enact our purpose. We want to be empowered to make decisions and allowed to figure out how to work smart. We want the freedom to do things in ways that support our values. We want to learn along the way, to become competent and able to fully accomplish our daily tasks to our own high standards. Ultimately, we want to become masterful. We want to do all of this in the company of people we like and respect—and who return the sentiments.[14]

To be happy at work, we need to make a difference. We need to be consciously attending to and enacting what we find to be inherently worthwhile—our values and beliefs. These will be different for every person, and they're often very private because they are derived from our upbringing and the culture of our families and communities. It may seem difficult—even dangerous—to bring such personal aspects of ourselves to work. I think, though, that fear has pushed us too far toward trying to keep our personal values out of the workplace. This is not usually possible, anyway: values tend to show up in how we work. We are better off if we can find a way to incorporate what we care about into our day-to-day work.

Transforming Personal Values So They Work at Work

Nikki Deskovich is the vice president of talent management and organizational effectiveness at Eaton, a global power management company. She finds her job deeply satisfying, in part because she is able to see a link between a core, personal value and her daily activities.[15]

Nikki hates waste. "I recycled long before it was popular, bought a hybrid car as soon as they came out, and I always try to be as efficient as possible so I don't waste my own or other people's time." More than anything, though, Nikki hates to see human potential squandered. She believes it's her responsibility to help people discover who and what they can be.

As part of her job, Nikki helps people make career choices that benefit them personally while helping the company, too. This isn't always easy. However, when acting from our values, we often find the courage to take a chance—to step out of the ordinary response to a problem and look for a solution that will be better for everyone. This is what Nikki did with a person she coached a few years ago.

This man was good at his job, and the company was perfectly happy for him to remain in a role that he felt he'd outgrown. He was bored, sure, but he was fine with staying put because, as Nikki explains, "He didn't think he was cut out for something bigger, especially a leadership role." He had settled.

Some talent managers would have seen this as a win-win: the company was getting what it needed, and the man was comfortable, even if the role had become "just a job" to him. Nikki helped him see, however, that by choosing to plateau, he was shortchanging himself and that a company suffers in the long run when people's talents are wasted. They spent many hours working through the pluses and minuses of seeking a promotion. Through these conversations, he came to understand that he wasn't satisfied coming to work every day to just do the job and he was becoming demoralized. Ultimately, he took the risk. He applied for—and got—a transfer to another division where he'd have the opportunity to move up and grow as a leader.

Nikki recently received an email from him with the news that he'd gotten yet another promotion and that he was truly happy with his new career. Before working with her, he wrote, he'd never even considered a senior leadership role and hadn't wanted to take the risk of shifting to an entirely new area of the business. She had helped him find his calling.

Nikki's impact on this man's life was the direct result of her belief that no one should waste their time, their talents, or their lives. Expressing this value at work helps her experience *her* work as a calling. Putting values and purpose first also helps her to be a better leader; in helping others reach their potential, she helps the company overall.

Learn How to Bring Your Values to Work—Without Getting Yourself in Trouble

What Nikki did—expressing personal values at work—is not always easy to do. Sometimes our values don't align with our organization's values, so we have to make a calculation about which values we can bring—and which we can't.

Deciding which values to share and which to keep to ourselves requires understanding others' beliefs. We don't all hold the same truths to be self-evident, and if we were to insist on sharing everything, or insist that everyone see things as we do, we wouldn't get a lot done because we'd constantly be in conflict over whose beliefs should be paramount, whose subservient. But we also can't pretend these differences don't exist. Talking about our values helps us to understand one another and work better together. It also helps us to create environments where everyone feels respected.

Still, the reality is that sometimes, we and our values just don't fit in certain workplaces. That's where social awareness comes in. We've got to be able to read people, cultures, and organizations in order to understand how—or if—we can bring our values to work. This is particularly important when we are looking for a job with a new company, and, unfortunately, it's something we often ignore.

I once joined a company because it was prestigious and reputed to be top in the industry. I was honored that it wanted me. But I had stars in my eyes, and I quickly found out that I'd made a big mistake. I simply didn't agree with many of the fundamental values that drove the people in the company. I didn't like the way people were treated (myself included). The hypercompetitiveness among managers seemed destructive. I thought I could just leave my values at home, and I faked it for a while, but I became increasingly unhappy. I eventually quit. If I hadn't, I probably would've been fired.

Leaving a job where there is a mismatch in values isn't always the only—or right—solution. If you want to bring more of your core self—your core values—to work, there are two things you can do. First, figure out what you care most about. One way to begin this process is to reflect on what you get excited about, what makes you proud. You can also spot values by examining what makes you uncomfortable or what makes you feel as if you are compromising in a way that does not feel good.

Next, examine your values and compare them with what we call "universal values." Universal values are those that most people, in most parts of the world, would agree are important and fundamental to a happy life. Honesty, integrity, compassion, fairness, respect, loyalty, responsibility, trustworthiness, generosity, freedom, and democracy usually make the list.[16] Surely, some of your personal values fit with one or more of these, and hopefully your organization supports many of them. Your task, then, is to use your social awareness to read your environment and put the puzzle together. This will help you discover which of your personal values align with those of the organization—and which really do not.

Both Josh and Nikki have learned how to transform their personal values into behaviors that have positive impact on the people they care about, employees, clients, and their companies. As Josh puts it, "I try to approach everything I do with an intention of creating the biggest impact in the moment for myself and for the people with me, and in turn, myself. If I'm with my kids and I'm coaching their team, I remind myself of my intentions: 'Do all the kids leave having had fun? Have they learned something?' The same applies at work. When I see people walking in in the morning, do they look excited about what's possible today? When I see them during the day, do they seem to be gaining energy and feeling empowered? And when they leave, do they look like they feel they have made a difference?"

There's another theme in Nikki's and Josh's stories, too: having an impact on something or someone we care about. When you can live your values *and* you know you're making a difference, your work has that much more meaning.

The Power of Positive Impact: Making a Difference at Work

My friend Mark McCord-Amasis is the vice president of real estate and facilities for the R&D divisions of GlaxoSmithKline (GSK).[17] The science of drug development has changed dramatically in the last few decades, but in many companies, R&D facilities haven't kept pace. GSK was no different, and it was time to move decisively to design research space that fit how scientists work today. Mark was asked to find a sustainable solution to this challenge.

Like Josh, he didn't jump immediately into action. Instead, he spoke with leaders, scientists, and lab technicians about what was working and what wasn't. He investigated historical approaches to lab design. He reviewed studies on how people use space at GSK, looked at labs in adjacent fields, and reviewed real estate costs across the company. And he observed and assessed how scientists worked day to day in the laboratory environment.

Through this research, Mark discovered that the labs were designed to support researchers sitting at benches working alone. That's not how scientists work today. There is a great deal more technology—automation, for example. People now need to harvest large amounts of data and collaborate with other scientists to make sense of that information. Much of R&D is iterative in nature, requiring scientists to work in groups in an environment that supports a variety of technologies, flexible teamwork, and access to what they need when they need it.

In response to these changes, Mark and his team came up with an innovative lab design that became known as "SMART Labs"—a new approach to facility design.[18] "SMART Labs," Mark told me, "need to be a collaborative space that supported interdisciplinary work. They need to be flexible to adjust to a dynamic R&D environment. They need to be efficient, effective, and they need to be able to tell the story of what GSK is doing." It makes sense to inspire employees everywhere by making the science visible. In the new design, the labs would be in the central part of GSK's building with glass walls so employees could see the heart of the company—science in action.

Mark executed this vision carefully and thoughtfully, tending to the ever-important people side of change. "Space is very emotional for people," Mark says. He had to get buy-in from everyone, starting with senior management. This meant that he had to start by working with people to help them see that while they might have to give up that treasured private office, the benefits of the new design far outweighed the sacrifices. Mark accomplished this in a very practical way: he and his team launched demo projects that allowed influential leaders to try out the new labs before they committed. First, one hesitant leader tried the new space and liked it. Then, a prominent scientist had a good experience in a new lab as well.

Soon the word got out, and the demand for SMART Labs skyrocketed. The labs have been a success. "You can actually see significant change in how people behave, how people interact with one another, and also in the business processes," he explains.

Mark has visible evidence of his work; he can literally see SMART Labs at GSK, something he finds deeply gratifying. He knows he's made an important difference to the company's bottom line, helped thousands of people do their jobs better, and enabled scientists to develop drugs and products faster and more safely. All of this work has deep meaning for him. "At the end of every wrench, there's a patient," he says. For him, every piece of equipment, every room, and every person working to develop new drugs has the potential to improve the lives of millions of people, and he can help them get there.[19]

Mark is making a difference. He's having impact. And he's doing it while also supporting his company's mission. He's part of something bigger than himself.

Does Mission Matter to Our Sense of Purpose at Work?

People want to feel that their work is linked to a larger, noble purpose, like Mark's is, and that their company's mission is meaningful.[20] But often these missions don't inspire people the way leaders hope they will. Sometimes they do the opposite. This is because a lofty, distant organizational mission can't replace the need to live *our* values and have a *personal* impact on something that matters to us. And, too many companies say they stand for one thing but call on us to behave in ways that contradict the mission under pressure or in crises.

Take oil companies. They provide the world with energy. That's a good—even noble—thing. But when the pressure for profit creates a culture in which people are afraid to speak up, the dominoes fall. Consider the Deepwater Horizon disaster, one of the costliest oil spills in history.[21] The impact to the environment was immediately devastating; long term, there are sure to be lasting effects. The company's reputation was badly damaged, of course, while inside, employees struggled to explain what happened.

Even when a failure to live up to the mission doesn't result in a crisis, many companies place purpose after profit. What can we do? Quit? Most of us can't—or don't want to.

The solution is to find something to love in our company's mission. It's almost always possible to connect with an aspect of your company's mission or work that you admire. Most companies, even the most flawed or market driven, have at their very core a noble purpose—a reason for existing that is useful to society.

I remember a conversation with a colleague, "Jorge," a few years back. At the time, he worked for a food production company whose primary business was cultivating and selling vegetables to fast-food restaurants. The mission it touted had something to do with "feeding the world," which sounds great. However, Jorge was more than ambivalent about the value of fast food. He struggled with the disconnect and even thought about leaving his job. That was an unrealistic choice for him at the time, so he tried to find something that he could relate to, something that made him proud. Jorge recognized that his division was actually at the forefront of research on fertilizers that do less harm to the environment—and human beings. It was beginning to introduce new products to parts of the world where people were literally starving. Once he shifted his perspective to focus on what his division actually did, he found peace.

You can almost surely find some part of your company's mission that you can support or even celebrate—aspects of the mission that link to your values and make you feel that what you do matters. If, like Jorge, Nikki, Josh, and Mark, you are able to connect what you do with what your company—at its best—strives to do, then you will feel that your efforts are worthwhile and your work meaningful.

Practical Ways to Find Purpose in Your Work

What can you actually *do* to find more meaning? Here are some suggestions I've tried myself or learned from the people I've worked with over the years.

Make, Create, and Innovate

Human beings are inherently creative. We like to innovate, see new ways of doing things, and engage in activities that result in something that didn't exist before. For some people, that might be writing code for an app, creating a presentation, or developing a new product. Others build, paint, or design.

For many years, we've known that we care more about the quality of our work when we see the fruits of our labor than when we're told to move widgets from one part of a machine to another. Car manufacturers now know to celebrate completed automobiles, not just expect line workers to be satisfied with putting a screw in the left fender. This is exactly why Mark and his team at GSK redesigned the company's facilities so that lab space is designed so that all employees—from an administrative assistant to a senior executive—have a clear line of sight into the labs and therefore have daily exposure to the company's exciting, cutting-edge scientific research.

There's more than just creating something, however. We want to make things that will *last*. Duke University professor Dan Ariely proved the importance of creating things that last at work in a study he conducted about what makes work meaningful. The researchers asked two groups of people to build figures with Legos. In both tests, participants were paid decreasing amounts for each subsequent figure: $3 for the first one, $2.70 for the next one, and so on. One group's creations were stored under the table, to be disassembled at the end of the experiment, but the other group's figures were disassembled as soon as they'd been built. The group that knew their creations were going to last made eleven figures on average, while the second group made only seven before they quit.[22] As Ariely said when discussing the research, "These experiments clearly demonstrate what many of us have known intuitively for some time. Doing meaningful work is rewarding in itself, and we are willing to do more work for less pay when we feel our work has some sort of purpose, no matter how small."[23]

We find meaning in the act of creating something that has utility to others—something that will last. Here are several things you can do to serve your need to create at work:

- Keep your eyes open for opportunities to join a group that is exploring a new idea or trying to solve a problem. Consider volunteering to run a team to tackle a project that no one else has time to complete.

- Find a way to track accomplishments and even activities that link to your values and/or make you feel as if you are contributing to something important. It is best to do this in a form that you can visualize, not just a list.

- Experiment with developing new processes to get work done. Share your successes with colleagues and your boss when you feel you've got something that will make a big difference to people's ability to work efficiently and effectively.

- Think about an important project you've worked on this year. What changed because of your and others' efforts?

Fix Problems and Contribute to the Greater Good

Many of us enjoy fixing problems. And, virtually everyone takes great pride in finding solutions and making things work more smoothly, whether it's better organizing our work space, remedying a broken process, or repairing a damaged relationship. Here's how you can act on your values to fix things at work:

- Don't blame others for inefficient, broken work systems and processes. Don't curse the proverbial "them" or wait for someone else to fix everything. They won't. You can.

- Don't be resigned to the way things have always been. Accept that most organizations are rife with old, worn-out, and inefficient processes and pick some to fix. Ask yourself: "What's the problem? What do I have some control over? What piece of a big problem do I touch directly? Where can I take action?" Generally speaking, no one will give you the authority to fix everything around you. But most of us have a lot more control than we think we do, and we have a lot more latitude to take action, too.

- Start small. You may not be able to fix an entire, convoluted budgeting process, but maybe you can change one report or form that will make your—and everyone else's—life better. One of my colleagues at a large academic institution inherited a nonsensical financial management system that made it impossible to track expenditures during the year. She couldn't change the institution's accounting system or influence her division's finance office. But she found that by simply adding two categories and using existing budget codes, tracking became far more accurate. When you make small but important changes like this, others will often become inspired and dare to make their own small improvements as well.

Find Purpose in Resonant Relationships

The very act of helping or supporting people can counteract the feeling that we're toiling at a meaningless job. Because we're so rarely working alone anymore, positively engaging with people may be the easiest way to express our values at work. Resonant relationships make us feel good and get more done because we are connected to and respectful of one another.[24]

And the added benefit? People who give generously of themselves are actually more successful than those who sneak, connive, and take.[25] Altruism makes us happy, and it contributes to success, too.[26]

Engaging your emotional intelligence to build strong and powerful connections creates resonance in your relationships, on your team, and in your organization. You and the people around you will experience more positive relationships, and you'll all be more successful. Here are a few things you can do to build the kind of relationships that give your work meaning:

- Regularly ask yourself whether you are expressing your values in your relationships at work. Make a list of the values that you hold dear and that have a positive impact on others—kindness, trust, generosity—and make an effort to infuse your interactions with more. You can do this in ways that don't take much (if any) extra time: start an email with a warm greeting and a question about someone's weekend, family, or pet project; share information more widely than you "have" to if it will make people's work easier. When you ask someone, "How are you?" stop and listen to the answer. Even ask a follow-up question.

- Offer to help with unsavory tasks, not just the fun stuff (and don't ever signal that a task is beneath you). It may be hard to find the time to help others, but research shows that giving away your time to help someone else makes you feel less rushed.[27]

- Build up that proverbial emotional bank account: put more good stuff into your relationships than you take out as a result of stress, conflict, and misunderstandings.

On the Road to Mastery: Set and Achieve Learning Goals

You can also find meaning at work by setting and achieving learning goals. These are not the same as performance goals: they have to do with acquiring new knowledge or skills, getting better at something that you care about, and mastering your craft. They're inspiring because they're tied to what you find important, not what others tell you to be, to learn, or to do. Here are several things to try when setting learning goals:

- Take a look at your current projects. Is there something you can do to move beyond a just-get-it-done mentality and enable you to learn new skills? Or can you set your sights higher than usual and strive for a standard that will require you to really stretch?

- Identify one or two things that you want to learn more about. Choose things that will help you better express your values at work. Outside of work if necessary, invest time and energy in reading or talking with more experienced people and experts. Then, experiment. If it's really something new—a brand-new skill, for example—you're likely to make mistakes. Be kind to yourself when this happens. And be smart. Practice in a safe environment, not on that big, visible project.

- Find a friend at work with whom you can set goals, and keep each other accountable. When we do this with and for one another, not only do we strengthen our relationship, we increase the likelihood that we will indeed have an impact on people and even our company.

It's possible, and essential, to have a deep and personal connection to our work, no matter what we do. We can learn to direct our energy and our talents toward something that's meaningful to us—at work as much as in our personal lives. We can see our work as an expression of our most cherished values, and by acting on those values, we can have a positive impact on ourselves, the people we work with, our communities, and the world. This impact is within reach if we look for ways to innovate at work, seek out new ways of doing things, or volunteer to fix problems that others are unwilling to take on.

Purpose is powerful. When we experience our work as meaningful, life looks brighter. It is easier to see (and to tell people) why we do what we do, and it's also easier to stay the course even when things are difficult and challenging. Purpose guides our thoughts and actions in the present, *and* it guides us toward the future, too.

Personal Reflection and Mindful Practice

Living your values at work and having a positive impact on something or someone you care about contributes to your experience of deeply meaningful work. In these exercises, you will have the chance to increase your happiness by exploring your purpose.

Your Purpose and Your Organization's Values

Your goal may be to find a job in a company that shares *all* of your values. But that sort of company is very rare. Most of us are in a situation where we can live only some of our values and can have impact in some ways that are meaningful to us. A realistic goal, then, is to be part of a company that enables us to live our most important values, to act in a way that is fulfilling to us, most of the time. To determine where you are, try this exercise:

1. Find a written statement or list of your organization's values, if it exists. If it doesn't, review some of your leaders' speeches, talks, and other correspondence to employees. Take a look at the human resources policies and orientation process, too. Now, draft a list of your organization's espoused values: what it says it stands for.

2. Next, draft a list of the values that *actually* drive your organization. Some hints for how to tell what these "hidden" values include:

   • Observe how people communicate with one another in person, on the phone, and over email and text. What do they prioritize—completing tasks or caring for others? Are people considerate, engaging, rude, or abrupt?

- Reflect on how people at different levels interact with one another. Are people with more seniority or bigger titles given more respect or let off the hook more easily when they make mistakes? Or, are people treated more or less the same, no matter what job they have?

- Ask yourself: What is the real goal of my organization? Is it profit? Is it service and contribution? Is it innovation?

3. Now, compare your assessment of your organization's espoused and actual values with your values. Where are the similarities and differences? How do you feel about what you have discovered? What can you do to leverage similarities and mitigate conflicts between your and your company's values?

Discovering Your Calling in What You Are Doing Now

There's almost always something about what we do at work, our company's mission, or the people we work with that aligns with our noble purpose in life. But, it's not always easy to figure out what that is. Sometimes it's even harder to determine how to magnify the best parts of the job while minimizing those we don't like—or what's counter to our values. This exercise will help you find those aspects of your day-to-day job that make you proud to live your values at work, proud to have positive impact.

To discover how to experience your work as more meaningful, consider three things: what you actually do every day;

your relationships at work; and what you are collectively trying to achieve.

1. YOUR ACTUAL WORK. Call to mind a time in the recent past when you felt proud of what you'd done at work. Maybe you went above and beyond and did a better job than was really needed, and it felt great. Maybe you became engrossed in a task or a project to the point that you couldn't stop thinking about it and you couldn't wait to get back to it. Now, *analyze* this situation: What was it about the work that made you feel so good? Which of your values were enabled and allowed to come to the fore? What kind of impact did you have, and why is that important?

2. YOUR RELATIONSHIPS. Draw a map of your social world at work. Start by writing your name in the center of your map. Then, put the names of people you like close to you. Put the names of people you have difficult relationships (or those you don't trust) further away. Try to include as many people as possible. Now, choose a few people on both sides—those you have good relationships with and those you don't. For each person, write actions you have taken that were intended to help and support each of these individuals. Try to remember even small actions—a smile for that grumpy coworker every morning; (gladly) finishing the report for your colleague when he was down with the flu; connecting your boss with someone you know who shares her outside-of-work interests. Now, look for patterns in the actions you take with people you like and even those you don't care for as much. What do you really like to do for

and with people? What habits do you have that make you proud?

3. WHAT WE ARE TRYING TO DO IN THE WORLD. Most of us want to do something important and good for someone or something. What good is your organization trying to do? Start with the mission, if you like, but go further. What are some of your company's values that drive everyone, collectively, to have a positive impact? Make two lists. One list can include what you are trying to do for "outsiders." What are you trying to give to your customers? How are you trying to help and support the well-being of the communities where you work or where you sell your goods or services? How are you trying to support the natural environment, or where are you trying to rectify negative impact on the climate? The other list will include things you are collectively trying to do for "insiders." What are you committed to doing to ensure that all people are treated equally, for example?

Something in this review and analysis of what's important to you at work will hopefully strike a chord with you and make you feel as if you have a real opportunity to live your values every single day and to have a positive impact. So, now you can do part four of the exercise by writing about what you see when you look at what's important to you, starting with:

4. "For all the ups and downs of my job and my career, I can experience my work as a calling. The way I can do this, if I choose, is to focus on . . ."

CHAPTER 4

The Power of Hope

Optimism Sparks Action

Gina Boswell is general manager of Unilever's UK and Ireland business—the company's fourth-largest market and the "jewel in the crown" of the Dutch-Anglo consumer goods giant.[1] When Gina took over this division, Unilever was trying to decide what to do about one of its best-known marketing campaigns.

Several years before Gina joined the company, Unilever had taken on the advertising world when it launched a campaign for Dove, a brand that includes soaps, lotions, and other personal care products for women. The new ads on billboards and television shocked people. Gone were the very young, rail-thin models. In their place were confident, beautiful women of all sizes, colors, and ages.

The images were relatable: women saw themselves in the ads; men saw their loved ones and friends. Children saw their mothers, aunties, and grandmothers.[2] Finally, a company was challenging the long-held beliefs that women buy products that show how they should look, not as they actually look. The campaign was a massive success.

Other companies soon jumped on the all-women-are-beautiful bandwagon, making it harder to differentiate Dove products, so Gina and her team were on point to decide what to do to sustain the momentum. The question on the table was whether or not to stay with the original campaign: Should they continue trying to reach customers through the realistic images of women? Or was it time to try something new?

Gina felt that Unilever should stick to the message and continue to lead the revolution it had started. Her reasons were grounded in facts: sales were robust, and brand awareness had skyrocketed. Moreover, employees were proud to be part of such a revolutionary effort, as she was herself. She believed that all in all, the campaign still had a lot to offer.

This business decision became more meaningful and highly personal for Gina when, to her dismay and surprise, her daughter began to struggle with an eating disorder. Gina knew well that these disorders are often linked to young women's attempts to live up to society's unrealistic images of the female body, exactly what the Dove campaign was fighting to change.[3]

In the coming months, Gina's daughter found her way through this challenging and all-too-common illness. With her mother's support and the help of family and top-notch professionals, she charted a path to a healthy and happy life. Meanwhile, Gina became even more committed to finding ways to encourage women with the refrain, "You are beautiful and worthy. You can do and be anything." Empowering women by helping them feel strong and beautiful is how Gina intends to help make the world better for her daughters and for girls everywhere.

Gina's vision is rooted in her personal values and what she wants for her family and loved ones. But there's more. Gina is envisioning the kind of world she wants to see for everyone, and her work supports her to realize this dream. She said, "We need to start with what women need at the most basic level, which is to feel good about who we are. We need to feel good about our opportunities. We need to feel confident that we are worthwhile." Gina went on to say that when women begin to feel confident and worthy, they are able to look to the future for opportunities—to pull themselves up, seek education, and find new and better employment and advancement at work. With this vision at the forefront, she vowed to expand the Dove message and to look for other ways to support women in their lives and at work.

Realizing such a grand vision is difficult and takes time, but Gina's dream feeds her passion, intellect, and resilience. So with the same strength that she drew on when her daughter was ill, she focuses on possibilities rather than problems. "You can see the glass as half empty and say that the world's going to hell in a handbasket or you can choose hope and optimism. I'm proud to be working on something that is going to be part of the solution, something that is going to have an impact on so many lives. Bit by bit, if you remove the barriers for women, you can take the world to a better place," she said.

Gina's belief in a better future for women around the world inspires her every day—at home and at work. Hope fuels her desire to excel in her job, and her vision helps her guide employees as they push forward day to day and quarter to quarter, while also inspiring them to see how their personal hopes and dreams dovetail with where the company is going.

Hope is the starting point for creating a future that is better than today. It encourages us to dig deep down inside ourselves to find our most unique talents and gifts and to use all of our resources to help us along the way. Whatever difficulties we face—whether it's a health issue or a loss or a setback at work—the hope that tomorrow will be better is what helps us get up every morning, put one foot in front of the other, and carry on. And, when we believe that things will get better, they often do. That's because a hopeful, captivating, and personally compelling vision makes us feel strong, powerful, and in control. We are motivated to face up to our present challenges and even our fears and to take steps toward the future we want for ourselves and others.

Hope is at the heart of happiness at work, just as it is in life. In this chapter, I'll discuss why it's so important, starting with how hope affects our brains, behaviors, and outcomes. I'll talk about how we can cultivate hope by learning to be more optimistic, even when work and life are tough. Then, I will explain the elements of hope—a vision, paths to the future, and self-empowerment. You will see how hope changes the world and our lives at work, too. At the end of the chapter, I will turn to practical, concrete actions you can take to focus on hope as a way to become happier at work.

How Hope Works

Think about a project at work that you are passionately committed to—one that means a lot to you. Now imagine that you've recently made a decision to slow the project down—to get it right rather than just get it done. Your boss doesn't agree. He just wants it finished and isn't concerned about cutting corners. If you are like most people, you'll immediately feel defensive. Something you care about is under attack.

As you conjure up all the bad things that could happen, you get scared. You're mad, too, and you start to second-guess your decision. Then the mama or papa bear inside you comes out to protect everyone on your team. At this point, you are not thinking clearly, you can't easily access reason and rationality, and you probably won't make very good decisions about what to do. You're in the throes of an amygdala hijack—that state when the limbic brain (what some people call the reptilian brain) is in charge and your higher-order thought processes shut down.[4]

When we're angry or frightened, our thinking brain is essentially kidnapped and gagged by our limbic brain. In this state, we are guided by survival instincts. Our manager—or whoever is threatening us—begins to looks suspiciously like a saber-toothed tiger. We act to save ourselves and to hell with the consequences. This is when we are likely to do crazy things like yell, ice people out, or pick a fight.[5]

Fortunately, the exact opposite happens when we experience hope. Let's say that instead of telling you, "Just get that project done," your manager asks what you will accomplish by slowing down. You share your expectations for the impact the project can have, if it's done right. He's interested and sees the logic of your vision, so the two of you spend time problem solving. Now, you're hopeful, not scared. Your hopefulness actually helps you think more clearly. Your creativity is at the fore, as is your ability to adapt and change some of your goals. You come up with a plan to give your manager what he needs to make his boss happy, and you buy more time to do the project right.

Most of the time, we think of hope as something that happens as a result of what we think and how we feel. And, as the example shows, hope does indeed emerge from our feelings, thoughts, and interpretations of our experiences. But it also works the other way around: hope can change our brain chemistry and, hence, our feelings, thoughts, and actions. This happens in part because hope affects the human nervous system. With hope, the stress response diminishes: our breathing slows, muscles relax, and blood pressure drops. This has obvious physical benefits, and our immune system even functions better. The physiological changes linked to hope also help us manage our emotions, especially emotions like anger and frustration that push us into amygdala hijack. We put unreasonable fears to rest, begin to see humor in situations, and tap into enthusiasm and energy.[6]

When we are hopeful, then, we are better able to access our knowledge and intellect, use our emotional intelligence, and rely on our intuition. We are more open and willing to consider new and different ways to reach our goals and have the emotional wherewithal to deal with challenges and problems. Hope fuels courage, too, which allows us to take risks. When a few of those risks pay off, we feel more in control of our destiny. We are even more likely to see people's actions as positively motivated. And, when we are hopeful, people are more likely to be drawn to us.[7]

Hope is a powerful human experience. It helps us in every aspect of our lives, including what we do and accomplish at work—and how happy we are at work. When we are hopeful, we can see ourselves as more potent in the world and more able to have an impact on our future. How, then, can we become more hopeful? One way is to deliberately become more optimistic. Optimism is a crucial component of hope, and it's something we can learn.[8]

Optimism: A Component of Hope That We Can Learn

Optimism fuels hope and is linked to a host of positive benefits such as happiness, resilience, and the ability to handle stress productively. Those of us who approach life with optimism and a positive outlook suffer less from anxiety and depression, generally take better care of our health, recover more quickly from illnesses, and live longer. Optimistic people also see problems as temporary challenges to overcome, whereas pessimists often see problems as long term and unfixable.[9]

We often hear people described as fully one or the other—optimistic or pessimistic. We talk about it as if it's fixed and can't change, as if we are born one way or the other. Psychologists, however, believe that we are born with a slight tendency toward optimism or pessimism, but most of how we approach life and the future is learned.[10] Nature plays a small part in whether we see the glass as half full, but nurture—our lives and experiences—plays a much bigger role.

Learning to be more or less optimistic starts in childhood when our experiences begin to frame our expectations. Over time, we learn to anticipate happy endings or disappointments. This is why creating environments where children can expect their dreams to become reality is one of the greatest gifts a parent can give a child.

Throughout our lives, we continue to learn to see the present and the future as either ripe with possibilities or fraught with danger. By the time we are adults, our outlook—whether positive, cautious, or pessimistic—is a habit. It is like a favorite sweater: it feels comfortable and we wear it often.

The good news is that even people who tend to be more cautious and pessimistic can develop and enhance the capacity for having and sharing a positive outlook. One of the ways to do this is to train ourselves to think constructively about the past.[11]

Positive Memories Spark Optimism, Hope, and Confidence

Going back through your memories while being fully in the present and also thinking about the future is what scientists call "mental time travel."[12] This powerful human ability can trigger optimism and hope when we are intentional about which thoughts and memories we focus on.[13] Consider my own story: by the age of twenty-eight, I had three children, no money, and no prospects. I was working as a community activist and I loved it, but it was essentially volunteer work.

I was tired of being poor. But because I hadn't gone to college, I simply couldn't get a decent job—one that I liked and also paid a living wage. I knew I needed to go back to school, but I was

Activate Your Emotional Intelligence

Hope and optimism are like muscles: they get stronger and more agile as we use them. To build these muscles, reflect on the following two sets of questions.

Set One: Strengths and Memories Lead to Optimism and Hope

1. Consider three key strengths that have always seemed to help you a lot at work. Include at least one that is related to emotional intelligence.

2. Now, write some notes about how you are actively using these strengths in a difficult or exciting situation at work.

3. Finally, how could you use these strengths more to enhance the outcome of that situation?

Set Two: Shifting a Memory

1. Focus on a memory of a challenging work experience, perhaps an experience where you failed to meet your own or others' expectations.

2. Now, review your list of strengths from the questions in the first set. How did you employ these strengths in this situation? Try not to give in to self-criticism. You almost certainly tapped key strengths.

3. Finally, what makes you proud of yourself in this situation?

By answering these questions, you can begin to shift your assessment of and your feelings about this situation. The next time you think about what happened, try to start with this more positive view.

stuck in a negative loop: How would I pay for college? How could I possibly do the schoolwork with three children at home? Would I really be able to handle the academics after being out of school for so long?

I could've stayed stuck, but luckily I didn't. Slowly, I began to tap into memories of what I'd been like in high school. I remembered that I'd actually loved school. I enjoyed working hard, getting good grades, and being proud of what I had achieved. These memories helped me feel more hopeful about my current situation, and I realized that the things that had served me well in the past would likely serve me well again. I started believing that going back to school and getting my degree, all while still being a good mom, was actually a possibility.

And that's what I did. First, I enrolled in a community college. I loved it, and within two semesters, I committed to finding the money to go to a four-year program. I applied for scholarships and grants. I worked out my schedule so that I'd be home with the kids as much as possible. Thankfully, I had a lot of support, especially from my sister, Samantha, who moved six thousand miles to help me. College led me to graduate school, and off I went. I was able to achieve all of this in large part by remembering what had given me joy about being a student in the past.

Taking control of our memories is key to optimism and a more hopeful outlook. Naturally, we need to be a bit careful when looking at the past, as our memories can be faulty. But— and this is important—we can choose to view our memories through a positive lens or a negative one. This choice determines how we feel about ourselves in retrospect. Our stance also affects how we see ourselves today and what we believe the future holds.

Obsessing about all the things that went wrong in the past and imagining it will all happen again today or tomorrow affects your ability to think, to process feelings, and to act in ways that will help rather than hurt you. Taking a positive perspective, on the other hand, allows your memories to ignite constructive feelings about the future, which in turn permits you to focus on what's possible and plan how to get there. When you consciously direct your attention to your past accomplishments and successes, you cultivate optimism and increase the chances that you will see more creative possibilities in your short- and long-term future. This means you will have a better chance of turning those positive images into reality.

Optimism is powerful because of the way it makes us feel. But, the elation and excitement we experience when our outlook is positive are just the start of hope. From here, we can turn our attention to other key elements of hope: creating a vision, planning, and taking actions to make the future come alive.

Three Elements of Hope: Vision, Plans, and Self-Empowerment

When we are hopeful, we experience a general sense of well-being. In addition to this good feeling, hope includes three elements: a personal vision of the future, something that matters vitally to us; plans and the will to work hard to achieve goals; and self-empowerment—a belief in our own ability to make things happen.[14]

Your Personal Vision

The largest, most successful companies are full of idealists who dared to imagine they could do something new that no one's ever done before. Think about Oprah Winfrey or Mark Zuckerberg. Or, consider Sara Blakely and Spanx. Then there's Bill Gates, who started Microsoft with a vision that someday there would be a computer on every desk and in every home. This was revolutionary at the time—and extremely hopeful— but that vision is closer to reality than most people thought possible at the time.

It's not just people with familiar names who dream big and seek to make changes that matter. Without hard-working idealists in companies and towns worldwide, there'd be no stories about people finding a way from poverty to prosperity, from loneliness to a fulfilling, love-filled life. Without people like Gina Boswell at Unilever, we'd have no significant social change, no big, market-changing innovations. Idealists like Gina see a future that is worth fighting for, and they do something about it.

Idealists dare to dream.

Being an idealist prepares us to craft a full, robust vision of the future for our lives, including, but not limited to, our work. When you create a personal vision (as you will in chapter 6), you start by reflecting deeply on what matters most to you. Getting back in touch with your values and what you find meaningful in life and at work grounds you in who you really are, as well as who you hope to become. For most people, a personal vision includes aspects of personal life like our relationships, family, and lifestyle as well as health and well-being. It also includes aspects of life that feed our soul: learning, maybe, or making a difference in our community.

A personal vision includes work, too—what you love to do and the outcomes you want to achieve. Work, like life, is where we feel a sense of *teleos*: a purposeful progression toward something that matters. Work is where we can reach our potential—and realize our dreams. It's where we grow, create, and make an impact, where we use our intelligence, talents, and gifts.

When we talk about where people are in their careers, we often use metaphors like, "She's on the fast track." Or perhaps you think to yourself, "I'm ready for a big move." We use similar metaphors to describe what happens when people falter: "He's derailed," "She's plateaued," "He's gone as far as he can in this company." We use these descriptions for a reason: we are on a journey at work. We want to know that as we progress, things will get better.

A personal vision of the future that is grounded in what's important to you is the starting place for ensuring that your journey at work is fulfilling now and in the future. Such a vision is a guiding light that can inspire you and support happiness as you move toward your ideal work life. Your vision also prepares you to make practical plans to get there from here.

Your Plans and Pathways to the Future

The way we think when we are hopeful, scholars tell us, includes "pathways thinking."[15] Pathways thinking is just what it sounds like: imagining several paths toward the future. The paths we see ahead of us include steps we need to take to prepare, as well as goals and milestones. These are markers that help us to know that we are making progress. Pathways thinking also helps us to envision opportunities we may be able to take advantage of and anticipate obstacles and barriers we may encounter.

To bring this to life for yourself, think about something you'd like to see happen at work or in your career—something that fits with a dream you have about the life you'd like to live in the future. Maybe you want to become a senior manager in your company, or you'd like to be part of the new product development team. Maybe you even want to change careers.

Let's take becoming a senior leader as an example to illustrate how pathways thinking works. First, form an image in your mind of aspects of the role that you'd love: influencing people, maybe making strategic decisions, or being on a great team full of talented and smart people. Think too about what you'd get to do and how the role would make work feel meaningful and rich. This vision does two things: it sparks positive emotions, and it gives you clarity about where you want to be in the future.

Next, ask yourself what you might have to do or learn in order to get this new job. Do you need to get a graduate degree? Would more experience in finance or leading a large project make you more qualified for the role? Do you need more exposure to senior management in your company? These are possible paths to your goal that you can consider—paths that you can prepare yourself to take. Now, lay out a few goals along each path—milestones you think you need to hit on the way. As you do, mentally catalog personal resources—your experience and friends, for example—that can support you, as well as obstacles (like paying for graduate school) that you must overcome.

Creative, thoughtful plans make it more likely we will realize our dreams. But, having a plan, no matter how good it is, can be a problem if we allow ourselves to fixate on certain goals or on just one path to the future. The world just doesn't work like this, and neither do people. Situations change, crises occur, and even our personal visions shift over time. We need to be able to adapt, to shift our plans, and to change paths as the need arises, and all without losing faith in ourselves.

Self-Empowerment

Believing that we are potent actors in our lives and that we have the ability to have an impact on our present and our future is another element of hope. This is what scholars call agency thinking.[16] Agency thinking includes self-empowerment—believing that we have a reasonable amount of control over ourselves and events and being willing to take action to realize our dream. When we are self-empowered, we don't wait around for others to make things happen. We take charge of our lives and our dreams with confidence and strength. When we feel this way about ourselves, we take bold risks and are able to adapt our plans without losing sight of where we are going and why it matters to us.

When you tap into the belief that you can do something to turn your dream into reality, you're tapping into energy and resilience as well as creativity. These, along with the belief in your own power, will enable you to find ways to capitalize on opportunities and overcome obstacles as you reach for your goals.

Self-empowerment is an essential element of hope. It is also fragile. We will inevitably experience frustration, disappointments, and even failure as we reach for our dreams. And, the bigger the dream, the more likely we are to encounter real problems on the journey. When we face daunting challenges and major setbacks, we can become discouraged, even disillusioned. If we choose too many paths that turn out to be dead ends, we can begin to lose faith in ourselves. We might become more pessimistic or even begin to feel helpless. This is exactly the opposite of what's needed. Negativity and self-doubt can kill hope. If you want to reach for your dream, it's important to learn how to deal with intense feelings—especially those that make you want to quit and to give up on your vision of the future.

If you want to train your brain to manage your feelings as you chart and walk paths toward the future, Daniel Goleman suggests looking at what he calls "top-down" and "bottom-up" thinking.[17] Bottom-up thinking is letting your base emotions like fear, anger, or feeling threatened guide your thoughts and actions. Top-down thinking is the process of consciously monitoring and managing your thoughts and feelings so they serve you, rather than the other way around. The goal is to engage the top-down mind as much as possible. This will enable you to stay focused on your vision, adapt your plans as you go, and carry on.

Top-down thinking is linked to emotional self-control and willpower, too. Willpower allows us to bravely walk forward no matter what happens. It also helps us to tough it out when things aren't going our way and delay gratification in favor of achieving long-term goals. So, even when things aren't going our way, we remain driven and patient because we know it will be worth the effort and the wait.[18]

Believing in ourselves, crafting an optimistic and personal vision of the future, and making plans to get there adds up to hope. And hope can change the world.

Hope Changes the World

As I write this, my friend and colleague Lechesa Tsenoli is currently the deputy speaker of the National Assembly in the Parliament of the Republic of South Africa. In his twenty-plus years as an elected public representative, he has been working to build a new democracy in post-apartheid South Africa.[19]

During the apartheid years, he was a freedom fighter—a contributor to the abolition of the inequitable and evil structures that were crushing black and brown citizens. At the time, the idea of overthrowing this system seemed like an impossible dream. Segregation was absolute. Power and money were almost entirely in the hands of white citizens, the descendants of Dutch and English settlers. Citizens who were black or of Indian or South Asian descent (referred to as "coloreds") were denied basic human rights. They were largely cut off from proper education and from the world. Most were living in abject poverty in the rural areas or in sprawling townships like Soweto. Living conditions were horrendous.

Still, people found ways to enjoy life, laugh, learn, and love. This is, after all, what people do. We are incredibly resilient. And when we are oppressed, mistreated, or abused, we fight back for ourselves and our children.

Lechesa talks about what it was like during these years: "The system was designed to keep us down—and hopeless. And those in power were committed to holding us back. Strangely, they didn't see much wrong in what they were doing and even tried to convince us they were right. But we were fairly convinced that an alternative was possible, that things could get better."

This was a dangerous dream, for even the smallest hint of resistance was crushed. As discontent grew, the government responded by making it increasingly difficult for black people to access education, literature, and information. In particular, it became nearly impossible for black people to access accurate accounts of historical and current events. The fear was that such knowledge would give people hope and therefore the wherewithal to demand change.

This is exactly what happened. Groups that came together for seemingly innocuous activities—like poetry writing and book readings—shared smuggled literature, news from around the world, and accounts of other people in other countries who had fought oppression and won. "It was eye-opening for us—very exciting and absolutely fascinating. We got to see how others viewed what was going on in South Africa and that they believed what we knew to be true: the system was wrong and we were right," Lechesa said. This knowledge fueled the conviction that their dream was good and just. As Lechesa explains, "Our hopes grew from the connectedness that we had, knowing we were not on our own, and that others elsewhere knew about our struggles and they supported us. This planted many of the seeds of hope in our country."

As hope dawned, plans were created in villages and townships across the country. Lechesa and his peers organized and planned to create a democracy where freedom and justice would be for all, not just a few. They traveled the country with the support of people who believed and wanted to help but did not dare openly join the movement. "They were rightly fearful of being harassed, detained, even killed. But quietly, without being asked, they provided some of us a place to stay unnoticed, a place where we could get work done, sleep overnight, join them for breakfast, and then disappear," Lechesa said. And, he told me, "Despite all attempts to oppose our networks, they were there, always. This was exciting and hope-giving."

Fighting for a dream like theirs required tremendous sacrifices. At times, Lechesa was detained, as were many of his comrades. But even from behind bars, Lechesa was able to grow the movement.[20] During one memorable stay in detention, he convinced guards to let him have a newspaper every so often for a few hours. He and his fellow detainees would commit the reports to memory so they could share the hopeful, exciting news that the world was with them in condemning the apartheid system.

Lechesa explained to me that they also sustained hope through sharing stories of the ludicrous things that happened during the apartheid years and laughing together. He quoted a proverb from the Basotho people, *Lefu leholo ke ditsheho*, which translates to "The greatest disease is laughter." Laughter is contagious, he said, and when laughter is shared, joy, connection, and hope are, too.

Humor kept them focused on their vision of a world where absurd things that were normal in that time would not happen anymore. Take, for example, the black man who was asked by an Afrikaans policeman whether he was bilingual. The man answered that he spoke English and three African languages fluently. Since the man didn't mention the Afrikaans language, the policeman concluded, "You are not bilingual." Lechesa and his friends found this hilarious, because it underscored the stupidity of the system they were passionately working to change.

Many people would've said that Lechesa's dream of freedom was impossible. But he and many, many others worked hard and built both national and international support for their cause and the dream. They fought. And they won.

Hope was with them every step of the way. It enabled them to forge ahead, even when the future was frightening and the challenge huge. It is the same for us: hope inspires our dreams.

A hopeful, positive outlook can help us to consciously reach for our biggest, boldest dreams. But far too often, we don't do this in our lives or at work. I believe this has to do with the misguided notion that hope will blind us to reality. Nothing could be further from the truth.

There's No Such Thing as False Hope

Big dreams are the start of big change in our lives and our work. That's because our dreams have an impact on the choices we make and our daily priorities, too. But dreaming big can feel dangerous because we've been warned throughout our lives—by parents, well-meaning friends, mentors—to go for the sure thing, to minimize risks.

As a result, too many of us throw our dreams out the window and replace them with limited (and limiting) visions of the future. We let our fears, personal insecurities, and social programming determine how far to climb and how high to reach. Worse, I've encountered a surprising number of people who don't have any true aspirations at all.

The consequences of shortchanging our dreams are very real. Instead of dreaming of, and fighting for, good education for our children, we settle for less-than-adequate schools. We don't fight injustice, even when it bothers us. We tell ourselves our small efforts won't matter anyway, or we sit back and let others do the work and take the risks.

This happens in our working lives, too. We settle for money instead of having an impact on something we care about. We don't pursue a calling. Instead of holding on to a dream of becoming an entrepreneur or a senior leader, we settle for a comfortable—yet boring and ultimately unsatisfying—job.

Part of the reason we give up on our dreams is that pragmatism is lauded and idealism is discouraged, even scorned, especially in the workplace. Too many of us don't believe that we have the right to claim happiness and true fulfillment at work; that's for other parts of life. We are supposed to be practical and to pursue a safe path, one that will keep us employed and secure. We've been told that to aim for a big dream at work is simply setting ourselves up for disappointment and despair. Dreaming big, they say, is equivalent to false hope.

I don't believe there is such a thing as false hope. Hope is not a hazy, dreamlike state of mind. It's not a wild sense of euphoria that blinds us to the realities we face in the moment. Gina's hope for a future that is better for women and girls doesn't block out the reality of what women face today. Lechesa and the many others fighting apartheid didn't forget for a second what the real stakes were or ignore what had to be done to bring about changes. I most certainly didn't lose sight of the huge financial and family challenges I had to deal with as I pursued my education.

Hope is not magical thinking, and it's not fantasy. If you've got a dream and you're willing to plan, adapt, and work hard, there's a good chance you'll make it. *Doing* something about our dreams is what makes hope different from fantasies.

How You Can Create Hope and Happiness at Work

Consciously cultivating hope is critical if you want to be happy at work, and there are practical steps you can take. Here are a few that I've seen work.

Focus on Optimism and What's Right with the World—and You

By deliberately focusing our attention on what enables us to succeed (our strengths, for example), we can become more optimistic and, hence, more hopeful. Unfortunately, though, optimism is not cool these days.

Banish Pessimism

Negativity and pessimism rule in politics, economics, and organizations, while people with a can-do, sunny outlook are pilloried for being unrealistic idealists. In his 2013 book, journalist Gregg Easterbrook chronicles just how negative our culture and society have become.[21] He followed it up with an opinion piece in the *New York Times* pointing out how the 2016 US presidential campaign peddled negativity and pessimism as a way to woo voters; in many parts of the country, it worked.[22] Day-to-day life experiences back this up: "Breaking News" alerts constantly pop up on our phones, and the news is never good; we hear dire warnings of terror plots on television and see images of devastating wars, hurricanes, and typhoons on Snapchat. Outrage, fear, and gruesome pictures are a click away.

This is not helpful to the achievement of goals in life or at work and can keep us in a perpetual amygdala hijack. Just as optimism fuels the hope and energy needed to accomplish goals, pessimism causes us to give up before we even try. Think about Winnie the Pooh's friend Eeyore; maybe you know someone like this lovable but sad donkey. The Eeyores of the world expect the worst. In this state, it's hard to generate creative ideas about how to fix a problem. They'll often defend their stance, however, telling you they are realistic and you are not. But it is no more realistic to predict doom and gloom than it is to predict 100 percent success. And I've never met a pessimist who is happy at work.

But, if you've become a "catastrophe thinker," you're not alone. What can you do, then, to return to your natural optimism and leverage it to build hope at work?

Enhance and Practice Your Natural Optimism

Stopping the tide of pessimism takes effort, but it's worth it: a negative outlook on the future is not going to help you to be happy at work or anywhere else. You can start by looking at your past through a positive lens, focusing on your strengths, and paying attention to what's going well at work. Here are a few practical things you can do:

- Draw on memories of times in your life when you were most optimistic, most hopeful about the future. What supported your positive outlook? Focus on both internal conditions (like taking care of your health so you didn't get worn down) and external conditions (like having strong, supportive friends who encouraged you).

- Think about strengths you use at work. Now, reflect on your work history. Which of your strengths have consistently helped you move in the right direction?

- Reflect on aspects of your mind, body, heart, and spirit that are most important to you. Now, think about how these have supported you to attain your goals and reach for your dreams.

Now that you have prepared yourself to be more optimistic, practice reframing how you think about your current work situation. Basically, you have two choices: "I hate this job and the people I work with" or "There are parts that I love and some good people here, too."

If you find yourself in the first camp, it's hard to be hopeful. It might even be hard to get up every day. When you get to work, you're likely to be in a hurry to cross things off your list and get out of there as quickly as you can. Or, maybe you really like your job but feel so stressed and overwhelmed that it's impossible to truly enjoy your work.

Whatever the reason for your discontent, try this: at the end of each day, instead of rushing out of the office, take a few minutes to focus on what went well that day. When you catch yourself thinking about all the things you didn't get done or that didn't go well, think instead about what you learned, the positive impact you had on others, and something you are proud of. Think about something—anything—that made you happy, if only for a moment.

Creating a daily mental catalog of wins (even tiny ones) gives you the strength to plan for the future and gain even more small wins. Positive emotions also help your brain to open up. Reframing problems so they look like steps on the path to ultimate success makes us more confident, too. If you train yourself to think this way, you are better prepared to deal with the bad things that happen at work. So, when you are mistreated, make a mistake, or simply don't get enough done, you can avoid pessimism, even if your brain had previously become accustomed to it. Later, when you're faced with more nonsense at work, you can think to yourself, "I got through this before. I can get through it again."

Tackling challenges with optimism, hope, and resilience allows you to think about a vision for the future—your future.

Don't Expect Your Organization to Give You a Personal Vision

"There's no vision here. And there's no strategy, either." I have heard this countless times in companies around the world. I've also sat with senior leaders who are shocked, confused, and angry when they hear people say these things. But the reality is that organizational visions don't travel very far beyond the board-room. They are often bland, undistinguished, or even obviously disingenuous; rarely are they personally inspiring.

And if we can't see ourselves in our company's vision and strat-egy, we can easily become disengaged, apathetic, and cynical. We need to know that we and our companies are on a journey that matters. We want evidence that both our own personal vision and the organization's vision are truly driving choices, decisions, and the use of resources.

A healthy, effective organizational vision will call on everyone to aspire to something they care about, a vision of the future that is personally meaningful. Remember, though: an organization's vision cannot be a substitute for your personal vision. Your vision of the future includes far more: family; lifestyle; things you'd like to learn, see, and do; and what you want from work, too. It is not possible for your company, no matter how great it is, to craft this dream for you.

One more caution: even when you know what you want, it's easy to forgo your own personal vision and hopes for the future. This happens when you become consumed by work goals—your company's and your own.

Your Vision and Your Goals: Make Them Work for You

A powerful personal vision for the life we want to lead and the work we want to do shapes our choices. Having short- and medium-term goals can help us turn our vision into reality, in part because they focus our attention and our efforts. Accomplishing goals and hit-ting milestones is also very satisfying and can make us happy.

Making progress on goals feels good in the moment, and it can keep us motivated to continue the journey toward our dreams. Working toward goals during our workday boosts our mood and motivation, too.[23] For goals to work, though, certain conditions must be met.

First, goals must be clearly linked to a bigger picture—your big dream. This dream must be personally meaningful. It is usually multifaceted, often not completely clear, and something that might take a while to achieve. In this chapter, you've read about three such visions: Gina's dream of empowering women around the world; Lechesa's dream of a free and democratic South Africa; my dream of a better life for myself and my family. When we keep our vision front and center, we are more likely to craft goals that will help us get there and avoid those that are distracting.

Second, your goals need to be well constructed. Most often, we hear that goals should be achievable yet challenging, specific, concrete, time limited, and measurable. Think back to the thought experiment earlier in the chapter about taking on a more senior role. You might start by setting tangible goals such as, "Master technical skills required to take on a more senior role." This goal, while a good start, will be more helpful if you refine it. For example, you will want to specify which technical skills you need to master. With this level of specificity, you can set very clear subgoals, such as, "Identify a training program that will enable me to learn that specific technical skill and enroll within two months."

You may think it's not necessary to be this detailed. After all, you're energized and excited to move up, so won't you just do it? But the initial excitement about a big dream often wanes as the pressures of daily life take over. This kind of specificity will help you to stay the course and, in turn, feel good about the incremental progress you're making.

There's a downside to goals, however. In our hypercompetitive, achievement-oriented workplaces, setting and achieving goals has become the main event, not something we do on the road to something bigger and more meaningful. A narrow focus on goal attainment is so prevalent in our collective psyche that sometimes all we do is set and try to achieve small, measurable goals at work.[24] Success has come to be defined by many people—and many managers—as goal achievement, rather than movement toward a hopeful vision of a fulfilling future.

We're constantly trying to reach targets, finish the project, or hit the metrics. This is all well and good if these achievements are steps on the path to where we want to go. However, if we're ticking things off a to-do list, or if achieving goals becomes the end in and of itself, we easily become disenchanted and unhappy at work. Small wins begin to feel hollow. We don't reap the benefits from the deep sense of satisfaction, enhanced self-worth, and happiness that achievement can provide.

If you, like many people, find yourself rushing from one goal to the next at work, or if you are so obsessed with specific goals that you lose sight of your dreams, it may be time to take stock of what you really want. One way to do this is to learn to articulate what you are grateful for, every single day.

Gratitude Practices That Turn Us toward Hope

When we think about something—or someone—we are grateful for, our emotions become more positive very quickly. This, in turn, affects how hopeful we are about the future. Try this: bring to mind something that you are thankful to have in your life. Maybe it's your partner or your child. Maybe it's one of your friends at work, or the manager in your last job who taught you so much. Maybe you love your new job, or are proud of your team and the exciting, important project you're working on. Maybe you're even grateful for a difficult or sad experience like a missed opportunity at work that helped you grow.

Now, think more specifically, perhaps about conversations you've shared with the person you're grateful to have in your life, or that early success your team achieved. Recalling these memories makes your gratitude more concrete, and you'll more easily return to these positive thoughts later.

Take a few moments every day, ideally in the morning and the early evening, to reflect on what you're grateful for in life and at work. You may be thinking, "I don't have time for that!" But you do. These reflections take as little as thirty seconds. If you can manage three minutes before you get out of bed and a couple of minutes before you walk in the door after work, you will affect your brain chemistry for the better, encourage hope, and cultivate the resilience you need to deal with the many challenges you face at work.[25]

Your Hope Helps Everyone

Hope is the starting point for any and all important changes we make in our lives, including at work. We all want a future that is bright, to believe that tomorrow will be better than today for ourselves, our families, our communities, and the people we work with. And hope is contagious. So, when you articulate your sense of hope to others, they will start to feel the same way. They, in turn, will pass it on to others and back to you. This is the start of a resonant environment—one where people enjoy working together and care about one another.

Personal Reflection and Mindful Practice

This exercise will help you to focus your attention on aspects of your life and work that are important to you. As you reflect, you'll be connecting to what you care about now as well as what you hope for in the future.

Circles of Life

1. To begin this reflection, draw about seven or eight circles on paper or your computer. Now, inside each circle, write a word or a phrase for someone or something you love in your life. These are your Circles of Life.[26] For example, you might write the name of your partner in one circle; your children in another; you might write things like "Health," "Work," "Learning and Growth," "Spirituality," and so on.

2. Next, write some notes about why each Circle of Life means so much to you.

3. Now, write a few more notes that capture an image of how each Circle of Life might be better and more fulfilling in five to ten years.

4. Was it difficult for you to stay with your hopes and to dream big? Go back over your notes and see where pessimism or fatalism crept in, where it held you back from dreaming big. Ban it. Rewrite your notes to capture your *real* hopes for each Circle of Life.

5. Write some notes about how you, your loved ones, your colleagues, and your workplace would benefit if you realize your dreams.

Dreams, Plans, and People

Hope is essential for happiness and for realizing a future that makes life worthwhile. Remember, though, that dreams are not enough. You need plans and a belief in yourself. You also need help. To practice taking action on your dreams, choose a Circle of Life from the previous exercise and do the following:

1. Articulate your dream—that longed-for end state—as clearly as you can.

2. Now, identify two goals you need to achieve on the way to the dream. For example, let's say you've chosen your "Work" circle, and your dream is to be in a job that allows you to pursue your calling and have influence on your field, in a company with a culture that promotes growth. Possible goals on the way to this dream might be: complete an advanced degree in my chosen field because I want to, not because I feel I have to; create a "hot map" of all the companies in my field that have the kind of culture I want (of course, you will have to do research to get this information). Color prospective companies red for perfect, green for maybe, and dark blue for "no way."

3. Make a list of intellectual, emotional, relational, and other personal resources that will help you achieve your goals and move toward your vision. Try not to be humble.

4. Now, craft your people plan for achieving your dream.

- Make a table with two categories: the Faithful and the Willing. The Faithful are people in your life right now who truly want the best for you (it's OK if there aren't many). The Willing are people who want to help but who will draw the line if helping you becomes burdensome (they can truly help you; don't dismiss them). You might think that the next step is to figure out what these people can do for you. It's not. Figure out what you can do for *them*. Start by finding out what they hope for, what their dreams are. Giving first is the best way to ensure that you will get the help you need, too.

- Now add a third column in your table: the Dangerous. These are the people who will actively get in your way; maybe they've done so already. (Hint: at work, these people tend to be self-centered, power hungry, passive-aggressive, or outright destructive.) Write some notes about how you can protect yourself from these people. But, even as you do this, remember that they're human, too. So, if you're generous and kind, you may be surprised.

CHAPTER 5

Yes, You Do Need Friends at Work

Love and Your Tribe in the Workplace

A few years after the market crashed, Janet Duliga was appointed senior vice president of human resources at Sunglass Hut; you may be familiar with its small, bright stores in malls and airports.[1] It was a tough time in the economy, and most fast-moving consumer goods companies still hadn't recovered from the recession. This was not the case at Sunglass Hut. On the contrary, instead of the sluggish sales that most retailers were battling, the company was soaring. It didn't make sense. Why were people buying high-end sunglasses when the recession was still so fresh and people—and their bank accounts—were still so bruised?

Janet and Dan Nowlin, senior vice president of stores and operations, thought it might have something to do with the company's culture—what employees believed in, how they treated customers, and how they worked together. I thought they might be onto something, but I was curious—what elements of the culture helped people do so well in their jobs?

We organized a team and set out to answer these questions through dozens of interviews and an intriguing study of the company and its people. What we found bore out our predictions and more. First, wherever we went, people told us they weren't just selling sunglasses; they were making people feel great about themselves, while supporting what they considered to be a human right—great eyesight. Second, company values around learning and advancement made employees feel excited about the future and committed to making the company successful. What stood out most of all, however, was that employees believed *relationships* were the single most important factor in their individual and collective success.

I experienced this culture firsthand when I visited shops around the world. In each tiny store, the climate was energizing and entrepreneurial. Employees were warm and they treated every customer as if she'd just arrived at a friend's house. Trying on sunglasses was an adventure—enjoyable for the employee and customer alike. The goal was to send people out the door smiling and happy.

It was more than just how employees interacted with customers, though. It was also how they felt about one another and how they behaved. On Janet's team, for example, it didn't matter if your job was vice president, assistant, or intern. Whatever your role or level of responsibility, you could join any conversation, speak your mind, and be taken seriously. People looked out for each other. They shared time and resources generously, even when it meant sacrificing something personally. What struck me most powerfully was how much *fun* everyone was having. They laughed often and kept one another's spirits high, while also taking work responsibilities seriously and accomplishing a lot.

Across the company, the cultural rules of engagement included respecting one another, valuing differences, working hard, and doing everything possible to make work enjoyable. People clearly liked one another, and this translated into the ability to share real emotions, have honest conversations, and find ways to lighten the mood when things got tough. Self-serving behavior was taboo, and in its place was a firm commitment to collective goals.

Certainly, there were tensions between some people in the company. There always are. But on the whole, relationships were marked by trust, support, and camaraderie. Caring for one another was something you just *did* at work, and dynamic, friendly relationships were the norm. We heard over and over, "I love the people I work with!"

We had the answer to our question: Sunglass Hut was doing well in part because of strong, warm relationships and a powerful sense of belonging in the company. Friendships—not instrumental, task-oriented relationships—were at the heart of the company's resonant culture, a culture that supported risk taking, innovation, and results.[2]

In this chapter, I will show that having friends at work is critical. When we feel cared for—even loved, as one does in a friendship—and when we belong to a group that matters to us, we are generous with our time and talents because we're committed to *people*, not just the job or the company. You will also read about how to build the foundations for friendships in the workplace and how you can improve your relationships at work.

We Really Do Need Friends at Work

If you like the people you work with, you probably also like your job and your company. If you don't like them, or if relationships are tense or disrespectful, chances are you don't look forward to getting up every day to go to work. And it isn't just that it makes us happy to belong and to have friends. Good relationships lead to good outcomes. This is just as true at work as it is in our families, neighborhoods, and tribes.[3] Unfortunately, that's not what we've learned along the way.

When I ask people, "Do you need to be friends with people at work?" they usually hesitate. Then they rattle off reasons why it's a bad idea: "I've got to keep a distance or I won't be able to have the tough conversations," "I might get in trouble," or "You've got to have clear boundaries." A few come right out and say that it's dangerous to have friends at work.

Something funny happens, though, when I ask people to describe what they *do* want in their relationships at work:

"I have to like the people I work with."

"I want to be myself at work without being afraid that people will shut me out or shut me down."

"I can't take risks with people I don't trust, or when I know they don't care about me."

"I want to have fun at work. Sharing a laugh helps me deal with stress."

Clearly, there's a disconnect. We think we should have relationships that are distant, polite, and guarded. But we want much more than that. We want to feel safe to be ourselves, we want to enjoy one another, and we want to like people at work. We also want them to like us.

This seems like common sense to me—why wouldn't we want warm and friendly relationships with people we spend so much time with? Moreover, if we don't like people (or they don't like us), it's going to be hard to find common ground, making it even harder to work through disagreements and conflict. If we suspect that someone's out for themselves or trying to take advantage of us, we're not likely to share our ideas or resources. Instead, we will be on guard and hesitant to collaborate. This is not a recipe for success—a lesson David McWilliams learned early in his career.[4]

The Link between Friendships and Success

David has worked at two major financial services firms, seen one nearly implode, and helped the other rise from the ashes of the Great Recession. In both roles David led managers and was in charge of the thousands of financial advisors who provided information and investment strategies to the firms' clients. In these jobs, as in every job he's had in the twenty years I've known him, David has led with a signature strength: a focus on people and relationships. He talked about how he learned this early on from a mentor—a tough, no-nonsense office manager. No one would have called this man warm and fuzzy, but he understood the power of relationships at work.

A talent for investing money might get you in the client's door, he told David, but that is not enough. If people are going to trust you with their money, they want to know you will tell them the truth. They want to know you respect them and genuinely care about their needs and hopes.

Money is personal; it represents our success, and it enables us to feel secure about our own and our family's future. If clients think you're pretending to care about them, or that you are focused on your own success over theirs, they'll show you the door.

David took what he learned about how to treat clients and applied it to leading the financial advisors and the managers who reported directly to him. He recognized that what was true for customers is also true in the workplace: if employees suspect that someone doesn't respect or care about them or their goals, they will likely become self-protective. And, David knows, an instrumental approach to people always backfires eventually because it breeds distrust. Relationships like these don't help us to be effective. In fact, they sap our energy and drive people away—especially when times are tough and bad news is on the horizon.

What works, David says, are relationships based on mutual respect, genuine understanding of one another, and caring. You've got to build trust. You've got to hold yourself to high standards in values and ethics and assume others will do the same. If these conditions are in place, and people like you, then you've got a magic formula that will carry you through the good times and bad.

I hear this when I ask people what they want in their relationships at work. They also say that these qualities are even more important when we face a crisis, as David did some years back.

Leaders at his company had promised much-needed changes to employees across the business. Everyone was excited about the new technology they would get and the pay structure was going to be more equitable. Then, the market shifted and the changes had to be delayed—maybe indefinitely. As a senior manager, David understood the logic, but he knew his people would be devastated. He worried that the best associates would leave to join the competition. What was he going to tell them?

Many leaders have to share bad news with their people. What was different about this situation, however, was that the associates respected and trusted David. Trust and respect are conditions that ensured that David could be honest with associates and he knew they would believe him. He was able to share how he felt about the situation and treat them as adults who could see the dilemma and deal with disappointments. And because David had invested a lot in building good relationships, they knew and liked him, too. This, David says, is a bonus—a bonus that allows you to take the conversation to the next level and support people even when things are really difficult.

In this situation, he was able to let them know he understood their feelings and concerns, and he helped them turn their attention to the future. As he put it, in situations like this, "You have to make people feel that they belong to a group they can be proud of, even if it's hard to see a bright spot on the horizon. And, if it gets ugly (as it often does when a company is in crisis), don't sink to the lowest common denominator. Instead, act in a way that isn't going to hurt the people who might not be dealing well with the situation. Try to understand where they are coming from. At the least, you'll know what you're dealing with. At best, you can reach them and build a bridge."

David had created relationships that were strong and friendly *before* crisis hit. Trust was already there. So was respect. And people knew that he cared about them.

This is what happened at Sunglass Hut, too. Instead of running away from one another in the face of the sluggish and scary economy, people came together. Instead of hunkering down and competing, people joined forces. Instead of giving in to the pressure or succumbing to stress and misery, people found ways to have fun. They created a new kind of relationship at work—one that looks more like friendship than mere colleague-ship.

During the time we spent together, Janet and I spoke often about the qualities of workplace friendships that help make us happier and more successful at work. This is where Janet's perspective gets even more interesting. As she and I talked about what people need at work to be their best, she boldly said, "People need love."

Love at Work

Love? At work? We just don't *talk* about love in the workplace. But love—the kind of love founded in companionship, caring, and shared purpose—is the single most important factor influencing happiness in life.

George Vaillant, leader of a decades-long Harvard study of people over the course of their lives, puts it this way: "The 75 years and $20 million expended on the Grant Study points . . . to a straightforward five-word conclusion: 'Happiness is love. Full stop.'"[5]

One of the more surprising conclusions from the study is that positive relationships are linked to success—even financial success. Specifically, "the 58 men who scored highest on measurements of 'warm relationships' earned an average of $141,000 a year more at their peak salaries."[6]

This study followed a group of economically privileged white men, but love and warm relationships are, of course, important for women, people of all races, and across the economic spectrum, too. There have been studies done of inner-city youth, gifted children, and women, all telling us a great deal about what happens to people over the course of their lives, including and how love and warm relationships affect happiness.[7]

The love of family and friends is essential to our overall well-being. Similarly, caring relationships with colleagues at work enable us to thrive physically and psychologically. The positive emotions we feel in such relationships help us deal with stress, and we are even less likely to become depressed. When we feel love and warmth from others and experience a sense of safety and trust in our relationships, we are happier and able to achieve more—alone and together.[8]

Taking it one step further, love and positive relationships at work affect everything we say, do, and accomplish in life and at work. Most people are intuitively aware of this link. Today, science also tells us that when we experience the kind of love we feel in friendships, the kind of love we experience with valued companions, our relationships at work become a source of happiness, and we're more productive, too.[9]

Companionate Love

Professors Sigal Barsade of the Wharton School at the University of Pennsylvania and Olivia O'Neill at George Mason University shed light on the kind of love that helps us at work—what they call "companionate love." Companionate love includes feelings akin to affection, care, concern for others, and compassion.[10]

In one study, the team looked at workers in a long-term care facility and found that those who experienced companionate love at work were less often absent from work and less likely to experience burnout. There were other positive outcomes, too: their work performance improved, patients were more satisfied and in better moods, and there were fewer emergency room visits. Not surprisingly, families of the patients were more satisfied, too. Studies of more than 3,200 employees in seventeen organizations showed the same thing: when people experience companionate love at work, they are more satisfied, committed, and personally accountable for performance and results.[11]

We should be seeking to build loving, friendly relationships with our coworkers, not running away from them as we too often do. Sometimes, we are scared to even try to build the kind of relationships we want and need, in part because of the misguided notion that we are not supposed to or are not allowed to be close to the people we work with. Or, we go back to our desks and hide out because we are stressed or overwhelmed, instead of doing what will really help—reaching out to people who care about and love us.[12]

Connecting with people boosts our mood and our morale, and friendships provide us with the emotional and psychological

Activate Your Emotional Intelligence

Friends understand one another. To do this well, we need self-awareness and empathy—competencies that help us see our friends as they really are, not as we'd like them to be. We can very easily assume, for example, that our friends feel exactly as we do or share our opinions and reactions to people and situations. This isn't always the case, of course.

Knowing what's going on inside us is the first step to seeing people as they are. Then, we need empathy. To truly connect with someone, we need to recognize what they are feeling and why; we must be able to discern their thoughts and logic, too.

This exercise will give you some insights into how well you employ self-awareness and empathy to understand your friends at work.

1. Call to mind a person you care about at work, a person who also cares about you. Now, think about a time you've disagreed or found yourself in conflict with one another.

- What happened in this situation? What did you do that helped resolve the situation? What did you do that didn't help? How did you feel during and after? Why did you feel as you did, and what was driving you to behave as you did?

- Now, write some notes about your friend's perspective on the situation. What do you think your friend believed he or she did well? Not so well? How did your friend feel about this situation? How did he or she feel about you? And, what was motivating or driving him or her?

- Now, review your notes about your own and your friend's feelings, reactions, and motives. Where are they similar? Why are they similar? Where are they different? Why are they different?

- Finally, write some notes about how you can use this reflection to help you the next time you find yourself in a disagreement or in conflict with your friend or others at work.

strength to deal with whatever comes our way—whether an exciting opportunity, a challenge, or a crisis. On a practical level, being with people we care about—and who care about us—is a good start for getting and giving the help we need to do our jobs. And, being in the company of friends helps us experience a deep and satisfying sense of belonging—another key element of happiness.

Belonging: Our Tribe at Work

From the time we lived in small, nomadic bands, we've needed one another to survive. We still do. There's more to being part of a tribe, however, than finding food or protecting one another. We also have a deep human need to belong—to feel part of a group of people who share our values, hopes, and dreams.

To understand how important a sense of belonging is, we only have to look at what happens when people are pushed out of a group. When we are shunned or banished, we experience sadness, anger, and despair. When we find ourselves in a team or organization that doesn't want us or doesn't accept us for who we are, we live in a constant state of physiological arousal: fears take over, we're anxious, and we can even become depressed. Stress is constant and our physical and mental health suffer.[13]

I experienced how badly being shut out hurts in a job some years back. A colleague and I were in a tiresome battle over how to use resources. I'd tried to find common ground, but he wouldn't budge. Ultimately, we agreed that at my next meeting with our boss, I'd lay out our positions in an objective manner and get his input. I would have easily accepted a fair assessment and hoped for a reasonable compromise. Instead, what I got from my boss was, "He's been here a long time. He's part of us. You are not. We go with his plan." That stung.

Candice Reimers, the leader I introduced in chapter 1, dealt far better with a situation in one of her teams that involved similar insider-outsider issues.[14] The team members worked exceptionally well together. People respected one another and, because they'd worked together for quite some time, they knew how to maximize each person's strengths. They also knew how not to push each other's buttons.

Enter a new team member, a woman who brought much-needed skills to the project. She also brought her aggressive personality. She had a bad habit of interrupting people. She blocked others' ideas and didn't listen closely to what they were saying. Team members put up with it for a while and tried sending her signals. It didn't work, and before long, people were shutting her out. They avoided her whenever possible, ignored her contribution, and even held important meetings without her.

She was irritating everyone, even Candice. She didn't seem to fit in with this team; her approach was just too different.

Candice felt, however, that her job as the leader was to try to make this work. She saw, too, that under the bravado were excellent innovative ideas, something the team needed. She also realized that the more this person was pushed out, the worse she behaved, something Candice could relate to as a result of what she had learned in one of her first jobs.

Right out of college, Candice had taken a great job in a tough, male-dominated industry. She knew she could hold her own. And she was right—at first. She learned quickly and stepped up to each new challenge with energy and competence. She was a top contributor, and she shared credit generously, even when it was clear that her performance was driving the team's results.

Candice should've been a rising star. But she wasn't. Hardly anyone even noticed her outstanding contributions. She was ignored at meetings and overlooked for choice projects. The manager who had brought her into the company took her for granted. He also took credit for her work or attributed it to others. This bothered her a lot, especially given how hard she was working and how effective she actually was.

The isolation was painful, and before long, there were real, tangible consequences. Candice said, "I was working on a team that had a different set of values than I did. I wasn't learning what I'd hoped I would, and I didn't see a future for myself in the company. I was out of place. I didn't fit in. I was always having to prove myself. I'd get out of bed dreading going to work. I punched the clock. I did only what was needed and no more. This had repercussions for me personally, too. I'd always been active and athletic, and all of a sudden I didn't want to do the things I loved and my health suffered. I left the company after being there barely a year." Candice never forgot what it felt like to be the one no one really wants, the one who doesn't belong.

She took what she learned from this experience and applied it to the situation on the project team. She worked privately with the woman whom others had shunned to help her see why this was happening. She found gentle but clear ways to show her how she was stepping on team values and norms, and counseled her about the impact of her caustic style. Candice also pointed out that she was upsetting people, which, it turned out, this woman felt pretty bad about. Candice met with a few team members and asked them to give their colleague another chance. She called out behavior on both sides that didn't fit with the company's inclusive, creative culture. Candice also set up work in a way that would make the woman feel included and give others the space they needed, and she made it a point to support people as they began to build a new culture, one where everyone felt good about belonging to the team.

Of course, this kind of situation is not fixed overnight. Feelings of being "in" or "out" run deep. But, ultimately, they were able to create a unified and highly effective team where all felt they could genuinely be themselves without fear of being kicked out of the tribe.

Connection with others feels good, and it helps us do our jobs well. We thrive when we belong to groups where people care about, like, and respect us—and where we can give the same back in return. We want to feel that people we work with are *our* people, even if we come from different backgrounds and cultures.

We don't have room in our diverse organizations for shutting out people just because they are different from us. If we are going to be successful—and happy at work—we have to give up the notion that we all have to see eye to eye on everything. We don't and we won't: we've had different experiences, bring different knowledge and skills, and have different beliefs. This is far from a problem; it is the reason groups are more successful than individuals. So, instead of shutting out people who are different, we need to value them *for* their differences. Then, we need to try hard to find points of commonality.

Foundations of Friendship at Work

The love and belonging we experience in our friendships at work are essential for happiness. However, friendships don't just form magically. It takes time and effort to lay the foundations. To start, you can focus on trust, generosity, and fun.

Trust

"Sean" had to work with "Marit" in order to do his job. But Marit was hard to deal with and seemed to take every opportunity to make things difficult. For example, she'd agree to plans in meetings, but then never follow through. And, when they were expected to collaborate to produce something, she was nowhere to be found. But, when it was time to present to management, she'd show up and pretend she'd been the driving force on the projects.

The Downside of Belonging: Covering and Conformity

None of us want to work in places where people don't want us, or where we feel we are so different that we're not heard. So, a lot of us try to fit in; we try to look and act the same as everyone else. But when we have to conform, we can lose our unique talents. We become less likely to innovate and more likely to do things the same way they've always been done, even when those approaches don't work.[15] We also end up with inauthentic relationships.

According to a study of three thousand people, by Kenji Yoshino of New York University and Christie Smith of Deloitte, a vast majority of people feel the need to "cover" or minimize their differences at work. Women are coached not to talk about child care issues to avoid the "motherhood penalty." African Americans avoid one another so as not to be grouped and labeled. Not only women, the disabled, or nonwhites reported covering, however. Straight white men also reported the need to hide things like age, disabilities, and mental health issues.[16]

Bucking the trend can be hard. But covering and conformity are often impossible, like when we are trying to hide our gender or race. If we try to cover these things, we are in essence trying to wipe out core parts of our identity. The price is high: creativity, unique contributions, and innovation. When everyone's doing this, our relationships are shallow and not at all what any of us truly wants at work. Add to this the fact that when we are focused on conforming, we are far less likely to be original, and we've got problems in the workplace.[17]

Sean tried to talk with her, but she always shrugged it off with something like, "I didn't think we had finalized the plan," or "That's not how I remember it," or even "Our boss likes my presentation style, so I had to take the lead." Her excuses rang hollow. Soon Sean gave up. He couldn't rely on her and he didn't trust her.

Sean had a very different experience with his colleague "Desiree," with whom he had to collaborate on similar projects. Desiree had more experience than Sean, so when they first started working together, she often took the lead. She helped Sean learn along the way and gave him opportunities to try out his new skills. She never claimed more credit, even when she'd done more of the work. She went out of her way to make Sean look good, and she clearly had his best interests at heart. Sean jumped at the chance to join a project with Desiree; he trusted her as a person, and he knew he could count on her, too.

We trust people who we know care about us—people who will help us and be fair. Trust grows when we see that people walk the talk when it comes to their values, too. We want to know that people's ethics won't shift depending on the situation.

Trust is not just about values and integrity, however, and it's more than simply part of our moral code. It's also about being reliable and consistent—critical competencies at work. Trust is engendered in workplace relationships when we know our colleagues will follow through and do what they are supposed to do. We also want people's personalities, moods, attitudes, and behaviors to be consistent and reasonable.[18]

I once worked with a person who struggled with her manager because, as she put it, "I never knew whether I was getting the friendly, warm Marty or the stern, condescending Marty." She said that his facial expressions, body language, and persona would be completely different depending on what was happening at work and who was around. She suspected it had something to do with him feeling out of his depth in his job, so she tried to talk with him. That didn't work. The end result was that she didn't trust him, not even the warm side of him. If he could be two different people, how did she know which was real?

There are some very practical steps you can take to build trust with people at work. Obviously, do what you say you will do. Keep your word and your promises. Live your values, and be on guard when you feel pressured to take small steps across your line in the sand. It is far too easy to get comfortable on the wrong side of that line.

You can also focus on how you deal with power, especially your own. Power—whether it comes from your role as a manager or your ability to influence peers—makes it easy to violate our moral code. This happens because powerful people are often allowed to follow different rules and they can get away with things others can't. This can be very tempting, but it's not going to help you build trust. The best way to remain true to yourself and trustworthy is to regularly ask yourself, "Am I acting in a way that I can be proud of?"

There are a few more things that you must do to build trust in relationships. First, if there's a problem in the relationship, talk to the person directly, not to anyone else. You can also make it a habit to find out what bothers people at work and then do your best to fix it. And there is nothing like giving credit to signal trust. Keep in mind that if you're intentional about sharing credit, others are likely to follow suit.[19]

Generosity

Wharton School professor Adam Grant's research shows that givers, not takers, win in the end.[20] Generosity pays in career dividends, relationships, and happiness. The more you give at work, the more you get, even in the sometimes dog-eat-dog world of work.

This way of operating contradicts much of what we've learned about navigating the often-brutal environment in our organizations—environments that encourage us to exploit customers and coworkers to get ahead. Witness the Wells Fargo debacle, where managers created false accounts for unsuspecting customers as a way to hit unreasonable sales targets.[21]

Most of us wouldn't have stooped this low, of course. Yet, unfortunately, taking is a norm in many workplaces. Takers come in many forms: slackers, credit-grabbers, self-servers. These are the people who don't actively seek ways to help others and look out for themselves first.

As obviously bad as this kind of self-serving behavior is, taking can seem benign, in part because we are so used to the quid pro quo exchanges we all have with our colleagues. On the surface, these seem fine because there's the possibility of an equal exchange. But, as Amy Gallo at *Harvard Business Review* explains, these "mercenary relationships" are really about getting the most that we can from another person or group.[22] There's a constant calculation. What will it cost me to get what I need? Did I get cheated?

Unfortunately, we've elevated mercenary relationships to an art form: networking.[23] Networking is one of my least favorite words in the English language because of what it's come to mean: casting a wide net—in person and online—to create as many mercenary relationships as possible in order to get ahead in an organization or a career. It's gotten worse as we spend more and more time engaging with people over social media. Anyone who has anything to give, like jobs or opportunities, knows that online and in-person networks are often full of people who want something from you and don't give anything in return.

Mercenary relationships leave us feeling unappreciated at best and abused at worst. And, studies show that when we build connections with the express goal of personal advancement or self-service, we end up feeling bad about ourselves, even dirty.[24]

We can easily find ourselves caught up in these kinds of relationships. And, sometimes, we take more than we give because we are overloaded and stressed. At other times, we close ourselves off from giving—and may even become takers—because we've been giving too much for too long. This happens often in our hyperconnected 24/7 workplaces where every moment seems to be dedicated to talking, emailing, meeting, and collaborating.[25]

For all these reasons, we can find ourselves becoming takers, even if that's not our normal way of operating. It is worth the effort to shift back to giving, however, because generosity is going to support us far more when it comes to building good relationships with our colleagues. People want to be around those who share their time, knowledge, and support.

There are practical and simple ways to become a generous giver, the kind of person people want to be friends with. Try, for example, to find out what your colleagues like to do at work and help them find ways to do more of it. Or, introduce colleagues to people in your circle of friendships and relationships—people who may be able to help them do something like get a new job, find a good doctor, or even plan a vacation. And remember: saying thank you and complimenting people doesn't cost anything. Making people feel appreciated is worth its weight in gold.

One caution about generosity: there is evidence showing that in many organizations, a very small number of people are seen as prime givers, and everyone wants a piece of them. So, being a giver can backfire; it can contribute to burnout and can even leave us open to being taken advantage of. The key is to balance what we give and what we allow others to give to us; that way, generosity benefits all of us.[26]

Even with this caveat, however, generosity leads to good relationships at work. Giving, along with building trust, goes a long way toward creating a foundation for great relationships at work. Both also help us pave the way for another building block of friendships: fun.

Fun

Janet Duliga told me a story about how having fun at work is a great way to build resonance on a team. One Friday, two people on her team showed up in red tennis shoes. It really stood out when they were standing next to each other, partly because it's not something most people wear to work. People started joking around with them: Did they shop together? Did they call each other and plan what to wear? It was good-natured, and everyone had a laugh.

Janet wanted to keep the fun going, so she bought a pair of red shoes and agreed with the others that it would be fun to wear them the following Friday. Team members also wore them at a big company event that was held off-site, and even more people joined in the fun.

These shoes became a uniform of their own choosing—and soon it became a movement. Before long, the entire team owned red shoes, and people on other teams were wearing them too. The fun spread, and Red Shoe Friday became a tradition, something that strengthened bonds among team members and beyond. Even now, with several team members on other teams or in new companies, they send each other pictures in text threads. They're wearing red shoes to work alone and in groups, and the fun and authentic connections continue to be powerful and meaningful.

Laughter and fun are powerful forces at work. Laughter creates positive emotions, which are good for creativity and flow—that beautiful state when our feelings, thoughts, and actions come together and we do our best work.[27] Fun and laughter are a way to bond while also releasing tension. Janet puts it this way: "Fun creates this energy around whatever it is that's going on. When we're riffing on something like the red shoes, or we're laughing about something that happened, or we're being absurd, it's a release. Laughing together is like a steam valve, but instead of the energy going out, it's flowing into all of us. When we go back to our cubicles or offices, we are reenergized and relaxed. We can focus again, even better than we did before that bonding moment."

So how can you insert more fun and laughter into relationships with your coworkers? To start with, it helps to be lighthearted about work, even challenges. Check yourself when you get into that hard-driving task mode that we all know so well. If you spend the majority of your time head down, frowning and intense, people will stay away.

You can also begin to think about work more like play. It's usually not life and death, after all. So, look up. Smile. Joke around a bit, as you would with friends outside of work. Try gentle self-deprecation: poking light fun at yourself for a mistake or your quirkiness will put people at ease and make it safe for them to have fun with you. Of course, steer clear of off-color or offensive jokes that have no place at work. And avoid humor that involves ridicule. It will come back to bite you.

Trust, generosity, and fun help us to build warm, positive friendships in the workplace. And, though it takes time and thoughtful effort to lay this foundation, it pays off in the quality of our relationships at work. There's one stumbling block, however: many of us don't work in the same building and may not even be in the same country. Relationships in virtual space require extra care and attention.

The Physical Distance: Relationships in a Virtual World

These days we commonly work with people we never meet face-to-face. In 2014, a leadership survey found that 34 percent of leaders said that more than half of their company's employees worked remotely, and they expected that percentage to rise significantly.[28] Working on a far-flung team presents its own set of challenges: time zones, language barriers, and cultural differences. All of these things can make it difficult to get to know the people you work with. And when you only see someone's name in your inbox, without a face or a voice to connect it to, figuring out how to form a bond, much less a friendship, is hard.

One of the biggest obstacles in virtual working relationships is that we don't share a common identity and what Stanford University's Pamela Hinds calls a "shared context."[29] It's tougher to build a sense of belonging when you aren't physically located in the same place and when you use different tools, processes, and technology. We often don't share the same national culture, and we may well have different values, different ways of relating to one another, and different ways of working.

Fortunately, Hinds says these obstacles aren't insurmountable: "I've seen plenty of highly functional global teams that don't succumb to these pressures. They act as a unit, give one another the benefit of the doubt when things go wrong, and resolve issues promptly and constructively."[30]

You can build relationships with coworkers who don't sit in the same office as you, but it takes commitment and conscious effort. To start, avoid the temptation to engage in instrumental exchanges about tasks. Instead, make it a priority to get to know your colleagues. You can read about their cities, states, or countries, for example, and strike up a conversation. Or, take the time at the beginning of conference calls to talk about nonwork topics like the weather or upcoming vacations, or to share a laugh. Find easy-to-use informal technology that allows for spur-of-the-moment video connections. It's always better when we can see people.[31]

Forming warm, meaningful relationships at work is key to happiness and effectiveness, whether in person or virtually. But, you don't approach every kind of relationship in the same way. There's one type of relationship that deserves particular attention: your relationship with your boss.

You Can't—and Shouldn't— Be Friends with Everyone

At most workplaces, there are people we simply don't want to spend time with—people who lead with values we don't respect, people who mistreat us and others, people who take more than their share or who are downright nasty. There are also bullies and people who employ passive-aggressive tactics to get what they want. These are people you want to watch carefully—and sometimes steer clear of.

The Bully

Perhaps you have a colleague who makes snide comments about people or constantly puts others down. Or, maybe you've had a boss who leads by intimidation. These people abuse their power. They overshadow, dominate, harm, and blame others. They are scary, so scary that we sometimes let them get away with the equivalent of murder; we let them destroy people at work.

Why, you might wonder, do they act this way? I can sum it up in a word: *insecurity.* I might add another word, too: *pathological* insecurity. We are all insecure about something. But these people are insecure about everything. Every interaction is an attempt to prove how much better they are than everyone else. And, when bullies are questioned about their abilities or competence, when they sniff failure, or when something goes wrong, they lash out.

You have two choices with bullies: let them get away with it or find a way to stand up for yourself. Giving in to bullies doesn't make them stop. It emboldens them. If you decide you must push back, however, be sure to line up support and resources, especially if they have more power in the organization than you do.

The Passive-Aggressive Person

Passive-aggressive people often seem like givers: they act as if they are helpful, as if they are your friends. But they are nasty and dangerous. They say one thing, then do another. They are nice to your face and then talk behind your back. They act as if they care about you, then the minute someone more important shows up, they kick you to the curb.

If you want to know if someone's passive-aggressive, look out for subtle but persistent attempts to undermine you or prevent you from doing your job; compliments to your face (or to your boss) that have a barb or criticism embedded; and feeling you're often set up to take the blame for things when you know for sure it's not your fault. Probably the best way to know whether or not you are dealing with a passive-aggressive person is to tune in to your feelings: do you feel helpless in their presence? This is exactly what they are aiming for.

Trying to deal with these people is like shadow boxing. If you confront them about their behavior, they have every excuse in the book. They insist that everything's fine. They twist things around. They make you look bad. They even make it look as if you're crazy—that you are imagining things. The first step in dealing with a passive-aggressive person is to recognize that it's not all in your head.[32] You may be able to entice them to be more direct, but don't get your hopes up; passive-aggressiveness is often a way of life. So, be on guard. And be kind. That's sometimes the best defense of all.

That Special Relationship: You and Your Boss

It's typically easier to create friendships with peers. But, it is at least as, or perhaps more, important to have a good relationship with your boss. After all, your manager has more influence over your experience at work than any other person—and more control over your livelihood. Your boss controls important aspects of your work and personal life like your pay and bonus, what projects you are on, when and how long you go on vacation, where you work, even when you can eat and how much sleep you get during the week.

This power dynamic strikes a very deep chord for most of us. Our feelings about a person who has this much potential control over us can cause us to react very strongly, even blindly. We sometimes don't even see our bosses as human: we demonize them or treat them like gods. When this happens, our judgment is clouded. Understanding these dynamics is the first step to building a friendly relationship with your boss.

I Hate My Boss

Some years back, I worked for a toxic boss. He was ambitious to the point of desperation; nothing was going to get in the way of his agenda and his success. Maybe because of this, he was threatened by almost everyone, including me. He was the person who hired me, so his attitude was baffling. Did he really think I would show up and not try to do my best? Why was he always belittling my ideas? Soon we were at war with one another.

I was young and a bit over my head, so I take some responsibility for the situation. As our relationship worsened, my emotions were overpowering. I despised the man. He knew it, so he upped his attacks.

Anyone who has ever been in a similar situation knows that everything suffers when we work for someone we hate. To start with, we often become obsessed with the boss's shortcomings and faults. We think about them—maybe even talk about them—all the time. This, and all the fear, anger, and disdain that go along with it, interferes with our ability to think and perform on the job.

Fortunately, you can almost always do *something* to help yourself and possibly even make the relationship healthier—and friendlier. First, if your boss is indeed destructive, you need to defend yourself.

You can start by creating psychological boundaries that protect you from emotional damage. If the situation is untenable, you should think about leaving. That's what I had to do; my boss was truly toxic. More often, though, the situation isn't that bad.

So, before you quit, ask yourself some hard questions. Let's say your boss is not as competent as you'd like him to be. This is frustrating, but do you have to hate him? And are your expectations reasonable? It's not uncommon for us to want our bosses to be perfect. They are not. They have faults and shortcomings, just like us.

It's easy to project our own "stuff" on a boss. Do you, for example, secretly worry about your own ability to do your job and, instead of dealing with it, you call your boss insecure? Are you jealous of your boss? Or, are you stressed to the max, but rather than admit it, you tell others your boss is burned-out? Or, are you resisting authority because that's what you *always* do with people who have power over you?[33]

Finally, stop blaming and start creating a more positive relationship. When you respond with over-the-top negativity, you make the situation worse. People know when you don't respect them and will often respond in kind. So instead of treating your boss with disdain, return to the foundations of warm and meaningful relationships: build trust so your boss lets you do more, figure out what you can give your boss, and find ways to have a bit of fun together.

You have agency in the situation and can choose to focus more on what makes you happy about your job and less on what makes you miserable. You can choose which emotions you lean into—positive or negative.

I Love My Boss

Now let's look at the other side of the coin—when we idolize our boss. It feels a lot better than hate, but adoration blinds us to who they are and the impact of their behavior, just as hatred does. We make allowances and excuses for stupid errors. For example, we may choose to ignore our manager's unfair treatment of colleagues. Or, we may not fully consider the consequences of his tendency to give harsh and unhelpful feedback. We may even cover up his mistakes or unethical behavior. In the end, this serves no one.

When a manager and an employee are in this kind of relationship, others are left out. It looks like favoritism, and it usually is. Team spirit and that important sense of belonging is destroyed. People get mad—at you. They try to figure out how to knock you off your pedestal. And if you get knocked down, your boss will find another acolyte, and the whole unfortunate cycle starts over.

It can be worse, too, because some bosses become addicted to adulation. They begin to believe they are infallible. Some of these bosses like adoration so much they will do just about anything to keep it coming; that's when they become delusional.

Maybe most important of all, idolizing a powerful person is downright dangerous. I recently met with the dedicated leadership team at the US Holocaust Memorial Museum.[34] The historians and educators at the museum have created an intense experience that shows the insidious slide into hell that can happen over time when leaders are adored and are seen to do no wrong, when fears are fueled and lies are normalized. True, it's a long way from dictators and the world stage to your workplace, but the underlying human dynamics are not that different. When we find ourselves in a situation where we allow our boss to slide, or when we compromise our personal ethics "just a bit" for our beloved boss, we are headed for trouble.

A Special Note about Mental Illness at Work

We make jokes at work about people who are "crazy" or "off their rocker," but the reality is that mental health issues such as depression, narcissism, and borderline personality disorder are more common than most people think. According to the National Alliance on Mental Illness, one in five Americans experiences mental illness in any given year.[35] Obviously, many people who suffer from mental health issues lead productive lives at home and at work.

But, partly because of stigma and also because treatment is difficult to access and use, at any given time we are likely to be working with people who are suffering with untreated—and often serious—mental health issues. The tragedy here is that most of these problems go undiagnosed and people don't get the help they need.

Compassion ought to be our first response if we know—or suspect—that a colleague is dealing with a problem of this sort. People with mental health illnesses and conditions need help. They need friends, just as everyone else does. Too often we size people up, do some armchair diagnosis, and shut them out. This isn't fair to you or to them.[36]

But, you also have to protect yourself from negative consequences that can affect you at work. Take depression: emotions are contagious, so if you work with someone who's depressed, it's very easy to start feeling down yourself.[37] Or, if you fear someone's behavior will put your job or reputation at risk, you have to take precautions; make sure you aren't linked in a way that will be harmful to you.

Have a Healthy, Friendly Relationship with Your Boss

Given the strong responses that many of us have to our bosses, it's hard to even think about being friends with them. But you can. And you should. It's good for you, for them, and for business. Warm, positive relationships with your boss that are characterized by clearly articulated and shared values, mutual respect, and positive regard are helpful and healthy. As Karen Dillon, author of the *HBR Guide to Office Politics*, points out, there are perks to being friends with your boss. She writes: "If your boss considers you a pal, she's more likely to trust you with information, say yes to your vacation requests or a flexible work schedule, and perhaps most importantly, pick you for high-priority projects and assignments. After all, it's human nature to treat people you like better than those you don't."[38] This doesn't mean you should seek special privileges or favors. It means you (and hopefully your peers, too) should create a relationship founded on trust, respect, and fairness.

To create a friendly relationship with your boss, rely on your emotional intelligence. Think carefully about what you want and need from this relationship, and examine your feelings and your motives. Are you becoming friends because you genuinely want to get along so everyone can be more successful, or are you trying to develop a friendship because it will benefit you alone?

You'll also want to rely on your empathy—your ability to put yourself in another's shoes. For example, do you really understand the pressures your boss is experiencing from above? Doing so puts you in a better position to build a healthy relationship and to help.

Finally, don't push a friendship on your boss if he or she is hesitant. Both parties have to be willing and engaged. Go slowly, take small steps, and be patient as this could take time. By taking responsibility for your own feelings and actions, you signal that you are ready and willing to engage in a relationship that is less about power or projection and more about real and authentic connections between two people.

Now, let's turn our attention to what you can do with everyone—colleagues, bosses, and direct reports—to build healthier, friendlier relationships.

What You Can Do to Create More and Better Friendships at Work

It's time to get serious about building warm, authentic, respectful, nurturing, friendly relationships at work and finding the love you need. But this won't happen by accident. It takes deliberate effort to make and keep friends in the workplace.

Make Time and Take Time for Relationships

Many of us have very good intentions when it comes to building warm, positive, and productive relationships at work. But the sheer weight of everything we must get done often gets in the way. The minute there is any pressure—an urgent deadline, a shrinking budget—creating rewarding relationships is the first thing to fall off the list. But, that frazzled, overwhelmed feeling doesn't just take a toll on our productivity. It also damages relationships or prevents them from ever forming in the first place.

So, instead of constantly thinking, "I'm too busy!" make friendships at work a priority just like any other important part of a job. To start, look at your calendar at the beginning of each week and make sure you have some time blocked off so that you are available to talk with people or go out for impromptu coffees. Monitor your actions during the day to ensure you're not always in a meeting or engrossed in a task. On a virtual team, you might make yourself available on a messaging app or schedule virtual coffee breaks with people. Block out a few hours each month to reflect on your most important friendships and identify things you can do for those people that would further build trust and make them happy.

If you make a connection with one person, he or she is likely to talk about you in positive way; this helps with the general tone of the group. You don't have to socialize every day of the week, especially if you're an introvert. Be judicious and do what feels right to you.

Use Empathy to Build Friendships around Tasks

Friendships often grow around the work that needs to get done. So, you don't have to go out for a beer or dinner at the end of the day (introverts like me are probably rejoicing). Try chatting at the beginning or end of a meeting, or stopping sporadically to check in with people. Ask them how they're doing, how they feel the project is going, and what they're most excited about at work right now. Even short interactions over time will help people get to know you personally and forge trust. You don't have to work in the same office to do this; you can ask these questions or chat like this whenever you join a conference or video call.

To do this well, you need to use your emotional intelligence, especially empathy. Empathy enables you to figure out what people care about, what they're afraid of, and what they find exciting in a task or project. Empathy helps you to pay attention to people's body language rather than obsessing about what you're going to say; to ask people for feedback about how they perceive you rather than assuming you know; and to talk about how people feel rather than dismissing people's emotions as irrelevant or unimportant. This goes a long way toward forming genuine bonds with the people at work

Forgiveness and Compassion Support Friendships

None of us are perfect. And at work, our shortcomings are often magnified because of the stressful cultures of our organizations. It's important to go into this endeavor of making and keeping friends with an open mind and an attitude of compassion. Feeling concerned for the people you work with and being willing to help them is a powerful signal to people that you are someone to trust, like, and care for in return.

If the people around you engage in relationship-damaging behaviors, don't automatically dismiss them or return in kind. Don't judge or condemn. Try forgiving them instead. Take a breath, take a moment to step away from the situation, and give yourself or the other person a break. You'll often find a good intention underneath bad behavior.

Compassion, forgiveness, empathy, and effort are practical ways to build friendships at work. These relationships make us feel fulfilled—something we deserve and want at work. Such relationships, along with purpose and hope, contribute significantly to happiness.

Happiness, though, is not something we can take for granted. We have to work at it and make sure it doesn't fade or even vanish from our busy lives and hectic workplaces.

Personal Reflection and Mindful Practice

In this chapter, you've had a chance to think about all the reasons you don't have friends at work, and all the reasons you need them. These exercises allow you to examine your beliefs about friendships in the workplace. If you are like most people, you will see that some old ways of thinking about relationships at work need to be replaced with a new and more productive mindset.

Examining the Rules around Friendships at Work

In this reflection, you can chart what you've been trained to believe about having friends at work and how this affects you. Then, you can take actions to create the friendly relationships that will help you to be happy and more successful, too.

1. List all the reasons you can think of for not being friends with people at work. Now, choose the two reasons that affect you the most. For each of them, answer the following questions:

   • Why do you believe this about friendships at work? Where did your belief come from? Parents? Culture? Role models?

   • What evidence do you have from your own experience that supports this belief?

   • Now, ask the opposite: What in your personal experience shows that this belief is not helpful and may be harmful?

- In what ways is this belief serving you? In what ways is this belief getting in your way or even making you unhappy?

- If you were to give up this belief, what could you do to form better and more meaningful friendships at work? Why or why not?

Generosity and the Extra Mile

True friendships are not based on what we get from one another. They are based on what we give.

1. To begin this practice, find a quiet place to reflect and plan for a bit of uninterrupted time. Now, spend a while simply thinking about the people you work with. At first, let your mind wander. Think anything you like; allow your thoughts and feelings to flow freely.

2. Next, focus on two people: one whom you consider a friend and one who baffles or bothers you (don't choose a person you can't stand—that's for another day). In turn, think about these people's strengths, gifts, and talents. Reflect also on their "flat sides"—what they don't do well and what irritates you about them.

3. Now it's time to write. For each of these people, write a list of *what you give them* at work. Start with general things like "trust" or "benefit of the doubt." Next, call to mind interactions you've had with each of these people and write specifically what you gave them in these situations (for example, I helped him finish the project by doing that last analysis; I reviewed his team's work

before it went to the boss; I quickly read the conclusions in the report and added one item).

4. You've cataloged a lot of generosity in this exercise. No doubt there is a difference in how generous you are with your friend and with the person who bothers you. Most likely you could be more generous with *both* people. As an experiment, review your writing and note the ways in which you are generous most often (the frequency is a good indication that you like to do this). Commit to doing these things a bit more often with both people. Stick to it and keep a log. At the end of the month, reflect on your relationships. It's almost guaranteed they will get better.

CHAPTER 6

Hearing the Wake-up Call

Chart a Path to Happiness

Everyone faces trials and tribulations, sorrows and disappointments in life. And, even when we think we know what it takes to be happy at work—purpose, hope, friendships—things can go really wrong. We have little control over some events; good bosses move on, bad ones take their place. Companies are bought and sold, leaving us in a precarious position, or we don't get that promotion we wanted so badly. Often these big and not-very-good experiences are coupled with a constant stream of smaller problems that, over time, are harder and harder to deal with.

Maybe you've had a series of setbacks at work, at home, or with your health. Combined, it all feels overwhelming. Even minor issues, coupled with life's pace and stress, can be exhausting and rob you of the joy you used to feel at work. Or, perhaps your job doesn't satisfy you anymore. Your daily tasks annoy or bore you. You're cynical and negative and not that much fun to be around.

When this goes on for a long time, it's all too easy to find yourself on the wrong side of the happiness line.[1] This is exactly what happened to Dr. Srikala (Kala) Yedavally-Yellayi.[2]

Kala, a physician and faculty member at Oakland University William Beaumont School of Medicine, dealt with disappointments, compromises, and stress for several years until she had a striking wake-up call that made her aware of just how despondent she had become. In the end, though, Kala's story is one that teaches us about enlightenment and how to take control of happiness at work.

The Long March to Unhappiness

Kala woke up a few years ago to find that bit by bit she'd lost most of what she valued in her work as a physician and a medical educator. Many of her relationships at work were not satisfying, and she had little hope that things would change.

It had started with a logical compromise. Kala wanted to practice medicine and teach, and she wanted a schedule that would allow her to be with her children as much as possible. Most physicians are expected to work grueling hours, so Kala felt fortunate when she was offered a part-time faculty and clinical position where she was promised a good balance of practicing medicine and teaching.

Tiny warning bells went off not long after Kala took the job. For instance, her patient load gradually increased, leaving little time to advance her academic career. Kala was torn. She loved her patients, but she also saw herself as a medical educator, so having to put teaching and mentoring on the back burner was frustrating. As time went on, it became clear that she wasn't fully included in the academic aspects of the institution. She even sensed there were deliberate attempts to keep her away from the scholarly responsibilities she craved.

Once, for example, she was abruptly taken off a prestigious faculty committee without any discussion or forewarning. When she asked senior administrators why she wasn't being invited to meetings anymore, they told her that they didn't feel part-time employees should use their time this way. They as much as said that they didn't feel they had to accord her the same opportunities as her full-time peers. They even used Kala's part-time status as justification for not giving her a raise when everyone else received one. The subtext was that her choice to work part-time while raising her children was not acceptable.

Her patient load increased even more when she was asked to practice at a women's shelter—something she found very rewarding. The problem was that she was expected to see these patients in addition to the time she spent in other clinics. This meant that she was donating all those extra hours. To make it worse, leadership didn't even acknowledge what was happening in the women's shelter, even when the team won a major statewide award for its work with female patients.

The unfairness rankled, and she was demoralized. But, she thought, what choice did she have? She was committed to her patients and felt that leadership had her over a barrel.

Why did Kala stay in this job? She felt lucky to have part-time work in academic medicine and she loved her patients. But there was something else going on, too: Kala was caught in the boiling frog syndrome.[3] When you're in warm water and the heat's turned up slowly, you don't notice. You get used to it, whatever "it" is: being marginalized, unappreciated, treated unfairly, or taken for granted. The hot water feels normal, and we stay, even when it hurts.

As Kala explains it, "I thought I couldn't do better. They devalued me, so I devalued myself . . . I really stagnated as a person, as a professional. I didn't grow. I was a robot. I just went through the motions."

The last straw came when the administrators closed her clinic. She was appalled at the disregard for her patients, many of whom were elderly and unable to travel to the new location. To make matters worse, a new rotation schedule meant that there was no guarantee Kala would even get to see her own patients. "The last thing I cared about in my job was taken away," Kala told me. "It's like your arm is cut off. All of a sudden, there's a part of you that's gone and you're looking for it."

She'd already lost her dreams for her medical education career. Now she'd lost her patients. She had felt stuck for so long that she didn't have any hope that things would get better. She hadn't felt safe getting close to people at work, so in addition to everything else, she was isolated.

Kala ultimately decided she had to leave her job. At first, it felt great, but soon she was at loose ends. She was a *doctor*. She began to think that in order to do the work she loved, she would have to make the same kind of trade-offs she had in the past and put up with the same kind of treatment in the workplace. Even the thought of doing this again made her feel terrible.

You can't call what happened next "lucky," but it definitely ensured that Kala would never compromise her happiness again.

One beautiful bright Sunday, the family was preparing to go to the temple to mark the start of the holy Hindu holiday Dussera, Navaratri. Kala's teenage daughter was excited; she'd been practicing her dance for months. She left early to drive to a youth committee meeting and to take the fruits, flowers, and other things they'd prepared for the ceremony.

Twenty minutes later, Kala's sister phoned, warning that their normal route to the temple was shut down due to a bad accident. Sensing something, Kala's sister drove to the scene and found to her horror that her niece's car had rolled over and paramedics were using the Jaws of Life to pry it open. Kala rushed to the hospital as fast as she could and found her daughter conscious. The relief was overwhelming, until a few minutes later when her daughter said, "Mom, am I moving my feet? I can't dance if I can't move my legs."

Miraculously, Kala's daughter made a full recovery.

So did Kala. It took time, but she's made good on her vow to work in a way that allows her to be happy—and to live as she chooses.

Kala's story is not unusual. It's rarely one problem at work that leads us across the happiness line. More often, it's a combination of many smaller challenges, seemingly logical compromises, and unending pressure. What Kala did that's less common, however, was to listen to her inner voice and bravely take a stand on what she wanted from her work experience. In this chapter, I will talk about how we can learn to recognize the early warning signs that tell us all is not well at work. To start, I will discuss stress, the sacrifice syndrome, and the ineffective coping strategies we often adopt.[4] Then, I will talk about wake-up calls—those faint physical, emotional, and relational warning signs that tell us happiness is slipping away. I will then chart four stages of the journey from dissatisfaction to happiness at work. At the end of the chapter, you will have the opportunity to create a personal vision and to plan for happiness at work.

Stress: The Happiness Killer

Stress is a normal, healthy, physiological response that can be helpful, especially in situations where we need to protect ourselves from physical danger. When we perceive a threat, our brains react by triggering changes in our nervous system. Our muscles become tense. Our hearts beat faster in anticipation that we're going to need more oxygen and nutrients. Our bronchial airwaves expand. Our pupils dilute so we can see more around us. The small blood vessels close to our skin become tight and small so that we won't lose as much blood if we're cut or injured. Our cognitive processing is enhanced so we think faster—for a brief period of time. Essentially our bodies are getting ready to run or fight.[5]

These responses are helpful when we're facing real dangers such as a physical attack or a natural disaster. Unfortunately, our brains don't do a very good job of distinguishing this type of serious danger from the kinds of pressures and threats we experience at work. Overly competitive colleagues, too little time for what needs to get done, and poor leadership are just three of the many problems that can cause constant stress at work, which in turn causes physical, mental, and emotional problems.

Long-term acute stress leads to high blood pressure, heart problems, chronic infections, and an increased susceptibility to diabetes and even cancer. There is also a strong connection between stress and gastrointestinal issues, muscular and skeletal problems, restlessness day and night, and substance abuse.[6]

When we are stressed to the max, we often don't take time for family, friends, fun, exercise, or even sleep.[7] Everything takes a backseat to other more urgent concerns—like getting up and going to work to deal with the day-to-day struggles. But, when we cut out people and things we love, we often exacerbate stress. And when we skimp on sleep, we are in for real trouble.

I know people who bragged for decades, "I don't need much sleep; four hours is great!" Well, they were wrong. We need seven to eight hours, pretty much every night. If we don't get it, everything suffers: physical health, emotional well-being, cognition, and decision making. If we push through, night after night, week after week, without enough sleep, we can actually become unhinged (it's called sleep deprivation psychosis).[8]

Lack of sleep and stress can contribute to other mental health problems, too. For example, some people find themselves dealing with anxiety disorders. Others overuse sleep aids, pain medications, or alcohol. Some people get depressed—clinically depressed.[9]

Sadly, lots of people live in this depressed state—and go to work—to their own and their companies' detriment. Depression affects the US economy and health-care costs as much as heart disease and AIDS. It's one of the top three reasons people seek help from employee assistance programs, and with symptoms like fatigue, irritability, and inability to process information or make decisions, it most certainly affects our success at work. Obviously, depression is the antithesis of happiness.[10]

Stress, then, has profound effects on our physical and mental health. Taken to the extreme, we burn out. That extreme state is far too common, and in fact Arianna Huffington calls burnout "our civilization's disease."[11] In today's world, stress is something we all experience, and work often makes it worse. This happens in part because of the sheer amount of work we have to do. When our beliefs, hopes, and dreams are under attack, or when something we love at work is threatened, we react as if we are in physical danger. When these kinds of attacks are constant, stress is magnified to the point that it can seem like our job is killing us. In some cases, it might be.

Stress and the Sacrifice Syndrome

The low boil of normal stress—being late for a meeting, turning in a report late, working with a team that is too small to accomplish its goals—can leave us in a constant state of worry. Add to this general dissatisfaction with our jobs, thwarted purposes, dwindling hope, and tense relationships and you are in danger of slipping into what Richard Boyatzis and I call "the sacrifice syndrome."[12] This is especially true for those of us who take our work seriously and give a lot. We are the ones who become depleted most and soonest.

This is what happened to Kala. A doctor's job is literally about life and death and the pressure is immense. While she and many emotionally intelligent doctors do manage this intense stress well, it can take a toll over time.[13] And in Kala's situation, decisions were made that negatively affected her career, she experienced unfair treatment and disrespect, and her contributions were not fully acknowledged.

Threats to our values, to our self-image, and to what we care about most signal danger and trigger acute stress. For instance, when a nasty coworker doesn't invite you to a meeting, you might feel you are being shunned—again—and have the same kind of reaction you'd have if that coworker was about to hit you. Or, say someone criticizes your work publicly. That's enough to send your nervous system into high alert—and stay there. When you have a controlling boss, it feels as if your freedom, your success, and even your family are at risk.

Added together, the intensity of our jobs and the stress we experience as a result of threats to our emotional well-being can push us into the sacrifice syndrome. When we are in the grips of this syndrome, our bodies can't keep up with the threats, our minds don't work as they should, and emotionally we're a wreck. Still, we try harder, give more, and become even more stressed. We often revert to old mindsets and behaviors that we know don't work—the happiness traps we thought we'd overcome. We find ourselves bulldozing over people just to achieve our goals. We fret about money, worrying about getting fired and losing our salary even when that isn't a remote possibility. Or, we overconform and try to be perfect. We may even start to feel helpless to fix whatever's wrong with us or our work.

Or, take "Bruno," an operations manager for a high-end retail brand. His default response to stress was to just work harder. This may be the most seductive trap of all when we are gripped by the sacrifice syndrome, because it seems as if it might solve our problems. But that's not how it works.

Overwork Is a Trap, Not a Solution

Bruno really liked his job during the first couple of years. He enjoyed the challenges, had good relationships with his colleagues and bosses, and saw opportunities for learning and growth. Then the company hit tough times. Bruno found himself working outrageously long hours, but he and his team weren't delivering the same results. Tensions ran high on his team, and he found himself worrying all the time about what to do to make things better.

The owners of the company were scared; they didn't know how to compete in this new environment. They decided they had to focus on strategy and make some hard decisions. They closed ranks, and Bruno wasn't invited into the tiny club at the top.

Bruno's colleagues saw that he had been iced out. They, too, were stressed and not at their best and they stopped interacting with him. Even a good friend on his team decided it was in her best interest to distance herself from him. And if that wasn't enough, the exclusive group at the top took on a new set of investors who came up with several wrong-headed ideas about how to run the business. Bruno was forced to make changes that he felt would be detrimental to the company over the long term. He was isolated, disempowered, and fearful for himself and the company.

Bruno was experiencing a lot of pressure at work and was also the primary breadwinner in his family. It was just too much. Everything in his life started to look worse than it really was. He started worrying about losing his job, even though that wasn't an actual risk. He couldn't focus on positives, like the company still being in the black and his children doing well in school. His outlook was tainted, and his body and mind were worn down. Ultimately, Bruno's stress boiled over and affected his health and his relationships, too. Colleagues and his bosses now had real reasons to ignore his input: he was just too negative.

Like Bruno, my default response to stress is to work harder. Maybe you do this, too. We work unreasonably long hours. We don't take breaks. We answer emails, take calls at night and on weekends, and skip vacations.

Overwork is not a good coping mechanism for stress. It makes things worse as we ignore our relationships, cut out fun, and eat and sleep poorly. Working like this doesn't help us get more done; it does just the opposite. We are too tired and worn-out to do our jobs well. Our resources are depleted. We become frustrated more quickly. We are more pessimistic. Our judgment suffers, as do our interactions with others. We lose our sense of humor. We can't deal with conflict. And we're generally less equipped to deal with even minor upheavals in our lives.[14]

So if the consequences of stress, overwork, and the sacrifice syndrome are so bad, why don't we deal with them? One word: denial.

Denial Won't Fix It

Too many of us are in denial about the impact of stress on our effectiveness, our well-being, and our happiness. This happened to me, for sure. I spent years doing more, and more, and more, thinking that would fix everything. I ignored the big signs (health) and the little ones (general irritability with everyone) for far too long. I didn't hear the wake-up calls, even though I'd written about wake-up calls for *Harvard Business Review* in the past.[15] When I finally woke up, I wondered how this could have possibly happened to me.

What I realized was that my slip into unhappiness didn't happen overnight—nor did Kala's or Bruno's. For all of us, there were signs along the way that things weren't as we'd like them to be. But, like a lot of people, I put on blinders and tried to motor through. I ignored my feelings about the compromises I thought I had to accept and tried to hide what was happening from my coworkers, friends, and even family.

The good news is that if you listen carefully (as Kala, Bruno, and I finally did), your body, emotions, and relationships will give you clues that something needs to change long before you cross the happiness line. Tuning in to your wake-up calls *before* you're miserable is a skill that you can practice and get better at.

Hearing the Wake-up Call

Some people face the reality of their unhappy work situation only as a result of a heart attack, a broken relationship, or a tragedy. Don't wait that long. Instead, learn to tune in to the subtle, quiet messages that tell you to wake up, open your eyes, and see what's happening to you. Wake-up calls generally come in three forms: physical, emotional, and relational.[16]

Physical Wake-up Calls

When you're heading toward unhappiness, your body often tells you that something is wrong. These signals are different for everyone, of course, but common ones include:

- Eating too much or too little

- Difficulty sleeping or sleeping too much

- Chronic fatigue

- Gastrointestinal issues

- Headaches

- Neck and back problems

- Tightness in the chest

- Too many colds and other seasonal illnesses

- Onset or worsening of chronic health problems, such as higher blood pressure

- Not smiling or laughing as much as you used to

We sometimes try to explain away a physical wake-up call, telling ourselves that it's temporary or not that serious, and that feeling slightly unwell is just the price we pay for having a job like ours. We also try to explain away emotional wake-up calls.

Activate Your Emotional Intelligence

The human brain and body thrive when we engage in mindfulness practices—a few minutes of quiet reflection and deep breathing every day. These practices help us to be more self-aware as we learn to slow down, calm down, and tune in to what we are thinking, feeling, and experiencing physically.

Mindfulness also helps us with emotional self-control and stress management.[17]

Many people think that to benefit from mindfulness, we need to meditate for long periods of time every day. But, even just a few minutes of mindful practice on a regular basis can help a lot.[18] You can start by trying this:

1. Breathe deeply: four slow counts in, hold it for a few seconds, and four slow counts out.

2. Imagine yourself in a peaceful and beautiful place.

3. Try to think about something that makes you feel good: what you're grateful for, maybe a person you care about or something you are looking forward to. Your mind will wander at first, and you might feel anxious, elated, or excited. That's OK. Just notice your thoughts and feelings and come back to that peaceful place.

   It's best to practice mindfulness regularly, as in every day, maybe twice a day, but don't beat yourself up for missing days; just recommit to do it the next day.

Emotional Wake-up Calls

Emotional wake-up calls are subtle changes in your feelings, moods, and approach to your work and to your life. They often include:

- Seeing the glass as half-empty when you're normally a half-full kind of person

- Seeing even small problems as insurmountable obstacles

- Feeling sad more often than normal

- Having difficulty snapping out of a bad mood

- Feeling unappreciated and taken for granted

- Feeling exhausted at the idea of doing something new and different

- Believing that no matter what you do, it won't be enough

- Dreading your work

- Getting frustrated easily or having a short fuse

Lots of people miss these emotional wake-up calls because they dismiss their feelings as irrational or unimportant, or attribute their reactions to outside forces. We might say to ourselves, "Everybody feels like this sometimes" or "It's nothing. It will pass." Most common of all, we blame it on others: "Of course I'm angry. My boss is a jerk."

What's important when tuning in to your emotions and reactions is not the isolated moment, but the pattern. If you take a look at the bigger picture and notice that you're just not yourself anymore, that your normal optimism is clouded by cynicism, or that your signature enthusiasm is all but gone, you may be heading in the wrong direction. If you see that you are generally much more irritable and grumpy than usual, you might want to take a closer look at what's going on between you and others. That's where relational wake-up calls come in.

Relational Wake-up Calls

Relational wake-up calls usually happen at home first because that's where we feel safe to be ourselves. And, no matter how good we think we are at hiding our emotions, it's hard to do that in all areas of our lives. So even if you manage to cover up at work, you're probably not able to keep it up at home.

Susan David, a psychologist and author, writes about what commonly happens: We yell at our spouses and our kids because we are frustrated with something that has absolutely nothing to do with them. Over time, we become sarcastic and cynical with people we work with, too. It's as if our bottled-up emotions explode, or leak in destructive ways. We can't help it; our ability to manage our emotions is essentially gone.[19]

Here are some common relational wake-up calls:

- Most conversations (and emails) are terse and task oriented: "You pick up the kids and I'll get the groceries"; "I need the report by Friday."

- People say things like: "Are you OK?" "Are you mad at me?" Or, "You never listen to me anymore."

- You are not interested in getting to know your coworkers.

- People in your life and at work are distancing themselves from you.

- People get quiet when you enter a room.

- You find yourself disagreeing and fighting with people about minor things.

- You are prone to criticize or blame others.

- You overreact when people disappoint you.

- You can't remember when you last had a good time with coworkers—or anyone else.

These wake-up calls are also easy to miss because we tend to shut down and build ever-higher walls around us when we're busy and stressed. It also hurts to see people taking a step back and not wanting to spend time with us. So, we ignore the signs or blame others. Neither of these responses will help us chart a path to happiness and may make matters worse.

Paying attention to physical, emotional, and relational wake-up calls can help us recognize which side of the happiness line we are on. Once our eyes are open, we are ready to prepare ourselves to get back to the kind of work life we want. Let's return to our stories to see how listening to wake-up calls can help us get back on track.

Answering the Call

Kala, as you know, quit her job. She was at a loss, thinking she might have to compromise again in order to practice medicine. She knew she did not want to end up in another unhappy situation and was grappling with what to do.

I expect that Kala would have woken up and reclaimed the right to be happy at work even without the major wake-up call of her daughter's car accident. But the near tragedy pushed her into an even deeper reflection about life, family, and work. She became acutely aware of how precious life is, how important it is to not waste a moment (never mind years) at a job devoid of purpose, hope, and friendship. Kala saw clearly what the job had cost her. She vowed not to let it happen again. She took actions, too, starting with letting people in her circle know that she was ready for a new challenge—one that would allow her to pursue medical education.

Some months after the accident, a friend called to tell Kala about a job that seemed perfect. This time she entered with her eyes wide-open, her confidence intact, and her commitment to

putting a fulfilling work experience front and center. She nego-
tiated a role that fit her personal *and* professional goals. Once in
the job, she relied on lessons she'd learned about what makes a
workplace healthy and built friendships that resulted in her own
and others' success. When she spotted even a hint of trouble, she
spoke up. There would be no soul-destroying compromises this
time around. It had taken some time, but Kala had found her way
to a new and fulfilling era of life and career.

Bruno's situation took time, too. He was sidelined and disempowered, shut out from any and all important work and decisions.
He could not quit his job; it just wasn't an option. After a year
of this, something interesting happened: the company encountered the exact problems he'd predicted and almost went out of
business. The CEO was fired, as was Bruno's ex-friend—the one
who had shunned him. The chairman of the board took over for
a time and asked lots of questions of the remaining senior leaders.
Repeatedly, the answers showed that one person—Bruno—had
tried to steer the company in the right direction. Ultimately, the
chairman asked Bruno to take the lead on implementing some of
the initiatives he had been suggesting for almost a year.

Bruno's return to happiness was not simply the result of being
vindicated, however. It had more to do with how Bruno managed
his wake-up call. Like Kala, he didn't just return to business as
usual when the immediate problems were alleviated. Instead, and
as a first step, he tried to figure out how his responses to the situation might have made matters worse, not better. Then, he tried to
articulate lessons from his difficult experience that could help him
in the future.

A lot of Bruno's distress at work obviously had to do with
the ugly situation and his less-than-collegial coworkers. But he
also saw that he had played a role. He realized, for example,
that his emotional responses to what was going on at work had

not helped him or the situation. He owned up to the fact that some of his colleagues steered clear of him because of his short temper and stress. He also realized that negativity had become a habit—one that did not help him to think creatively or draw people to him. He recognized that he'd need to change his pessimistic outlook.

As a second step, he articulated what he liked about his work, even during the tough times. He also cataloged some of his strengths—those that had actually helped him to tough out a difficult year.

Third, he took a realistic look at his job and his company. He realized he needed to honestly assess his new job, including relationships with leaders and his coworkers. He asked questions like: Can this job provide me with the kind of work life I wanted? Would it be possible to be at my best and happy in this company, in this job? What can I do to shift my responsibilities and my attitude so I can find more meaning in the work I am doing?

Finally, Bruno crafted a plan for the future—a plan that included a compelling personal vision for himself as a person and a professional.

What Bruno did is a multistep process that we can use to turn a wake-up call into actions that help us on the journey back to happiness.

Four Stages of the Journey from Despair and Resignation to Happiness

Hearing a wake-up call is the beginning of your trek back to happiness. Let's now look at four stages of the journey from where you are now to a much better, happier you at work.

Stage One: Get Me the Hell Out of Here

Once you wake up to the fact that you're not happy, you're likely to be flooded with emotion. It's not fun, but in an odd sort of way, it can feel good, especially if you've been suppressing your emotions for a long time. But what do you *do* with all these feelings? It can be overwhelming, but stay with it. Emotional self-awareness is the first stage of awakening.

Emotional Self-Awareness

When you start to notice some of the difficult and even destructive emotions that have become habitual, you might react by trying to stuff those feelings away again. This is normal, but it's not productive. To counter that reaction, start by simply noticing when you want to push those feelings down with old excuses or when you start saying to yourself, "How I feel doesn't matter; I just need to get my work done." Don't minimize what you're going through ("Everyone has bad days"), blame yourself ("Other people are able to deal with a lot more. What's wrong with me?"), or think that your stress doesn't count because it's work related ("I should be able to just leave it at the office"). Instead, be honest with yourself about your feelings, thoughts, and reactions.

I call this letting your amygdala out for a walk—on a leash. Allow yourself to feel, really feel, those primal emotions. Maybe you're angry at others. More than likely you're angry at yourself. You feel hurt, and you feel you might have wasted a lot of time.

A caution: when you recognize and admit that you're unhappy at work, you might be inclined to make a big change—give up on your dreams, find a new business partner, tell your boss off, or quit your job. This is where emotional self-control comes in.

Emotional Self-Control

Most of the time you will need to find a way back to happiness *without* changing your job. Even if you think it might be time to leave, as Kala and I ultimately realized, it's a mistake to make decisions in amygdala hijack, when our limbic brain—not our rational brain—is calling the shots.

Emotional self-control is just what it sounds like: managing your feelings so they don't become destructive to you or others. You want to use your newfound anger, hurt, or even sadness to drive you to do the right things, like take care of your physical and mental health and rekindle relationships.

For example, if you've been ignoring your blood pressure, weight, or general fitness, commit to dealing with it and start (small) today. Take a walk. Sit quietly for a few minutes and breathe. Look at your calendar and cancel some appointments so you can go to the gym (or the doctor).

Or, if you have realized that you may be a little bit depressed or are dealing with other mental health problems (like overuse of alcohol or other substances), don't beat yourself up. That's likely going to make it worse. Instead, you may want to take a big step and recognize it's time to get help. This may be hard to do, as we've been conditioned to believe that having mental health problems is shameful. It's not. On the contrary, it's a normal response to an abnormal situation (working hard enough to kill yourself and being unhappy all the time). So, have compassion for yourself, take a deep breath, and reach out.

As you wake up to how you are really feeling and the consequences of long-term stress or unhappiness, it often helps to start by talking to a loved one or a friend about what you are feeling and what you are doing about it. Reaching out and rekindling a friendship is one of the best and fastest ways to start on a new path. With good friends, we can let it all out. They listen and help us move through our strong emotional reactions to a wake-up call. Friends can also help us rein in our more negative feelings and begin to change our mindset so we are ready to make changes.

Self-awareness and emotional self-control help us to understand what's going on with us and then manage our feelings so we can make the right decisions. When we're able to manage our emotions like this, we are more likely to activate hope and see a bright future. We can lean on another emotional intelligence competency to help us, too—positive outlook.

Positive Outlook

We all have narratives that we tell ourselves when we're under stress or in a difficult situation. And the tapes that play inside our head continue to roll even after a wake-up call. Many people start by blaming others for their unhappiness. Some people never get past that. You can. Try to look at the situation more objectively. Shifting your narratives from negative to positive can have a profound impact on your mental state, transforming feelings from lack of control to self-efficacy, and from overwhelmed to resilient.

As you learned in chapter 4, drawing on your memories is a good way to tap into hope and optimism, which provide psychological resilience and the ability to bounce back from negative circumstances. When we choose optimism over pessimism, the parts of our nervous system that are involved in the stress response begin to lose power and we're able to remain calm, energized, and focused. The practices that I talked about in chapter 4— gratitude, reflection on what's right—can help you weather a tough month or even a difficult year.

Stage Two: Figure Out What You Like and Hold Steady, Even When It's Tough

Murray Wigsten is, as I write this book, eighty-eight years old.[20] He's still working and he's happy. Murray is an antiques dealer; he buys old tools, toys, art, and what's called "primitive" furniture in the United Kingdom and Holland and sells it all at auctions in New England. It's not easy work. It is physical (he fixes and refinishes the objects before selling them), and there's no guarantee that he'll get what things are worth in an auction.

I asked him what the secret to being happy at work is and he told me, *"You've got to like what you do.* Work isn't always going to be fun, but there's got to be something, every day, that makes it feel worthwhile. Buying and selling antiques is risky. But it's an adventure, and I like adventure. I like going to new places— flea markets in rural England, little stores tucked away in small towns, even people's homes and barns. I like meeting people and I like talking to them. It's fun. And the stuff I buy and sell—it's terrific, it's beautiful, the people who made it were so clever. I also feel like it's worthwhile to save this stuff."

Making sure that his work links to what's important to him is a big part of why Murray likes what he does. But when we are stuck and unhappy, we can easily lose sight of what matters to us. If you're navigating through a wake-up call, it's critical to reconnect with what matters to you—your values and the impact you have on something that's important to you. Spend time figuring out what you care about and make sure you can do something linked to that *today*, something that makes you feel you are having positive impact *right now*.

By finding opportunities to act on what matters to you, you're doing two things: moving back to happiness and shoring up your resources so you can stay the course as you move to the future.

Moving from a wake-up call to a new work life takes time and can be tough. You've got to be patient. You've also got to be resilient.

Another friend, Charles Ramsey, shared good advice about how to hold steady when things are tough.[21] Charles recently retired as commissioner of the Philadelphia Police Department.

Chuck, as his friends call him, is not your stereotypical police leader. He defines "law enforcement" as "upholding constitutional rights." Among his many accomplishments, he was appointed by President Obama to lead task forces on law enforcement and gun control. Now, he's consulting to major cities on policing and the serious issues facing our communities today. He also leads the Police Executive Leadership Institute, which I am proud to be part of. The institute, which we developed with the Major Cities Chiefs Association and the US Holocaust Memorial Museum, prepares the best up-and-coming police executives for the top jobs in North America's largest cities.[22] In essence, the program helps these talented individuals lead differently from the historical norm in policing, while changing the institutions' cultures and place in our communities.

Chuck was police chief in Washington, DC, during the 9/11 attacks, the anthrax crisis, and the DC sniper case—some of the toughest situations a police leader could face. But in a profession like policing, even normal day-to-day work is tough. Everyone, from new recruits to senior leaders, sees and hears about the worst humanity can offer, every single day. When I asked Chuck how he dealt with it, he said two things. First, and similar to what Murray Wigsten expressed, he said, "You've got to like what you do. You've got to find meaning in it and you have to feel that what you do will make a difference."

Then he said something else that caught my attention: "Sometimes, you just have to keep going. Some days, you don't want to get out of bed. You want to quit. You want to be done with it. But you can't. You've got to steel yourself and just keep going."

It's true. There are times when we have to manage our urge to run away. We just have to stick it out. Work is not always going to be fun, or good, or a happy place. That's unrealistic to expect. But, as Chuck said, "You've also got to be careful not to shut down, not to bury your emotions forever. It's tempting, especially if you see the kinds of things we see. But if you shut down, problems will crop up—at work and at home." He went on to add that you can't continually dwell on the negatives. You have to turn your attention to aspects of the day-to-day that make you feel good about yourself and your team.

Charting a path to happiness at work means focusing not on what makes you miserable but on what you like to do, the kind of people you want to work with, and the kind of company that inspires you, even if things aren't always perfect. Being clear about your purpose, finding a hopeful, optimistic view of the future at work, and building the kind of friendships that you want at work are the key to understanding what you like about your current job—or what you must seek in a new one.

Remember, you won't be happy in a job that doesn't allow you to be who you are, or to pursue meaning and to have impact in a way that makes you feel that your efforts are worthwhile. It's either time to change how you see the job and your work or time to find a new job. The only way you can know the difference is if you take stock—honestly and objectively—of your current situation.

Stage Three: Honestly Assess Your Work Situation

People, culture, and systems at work have the power to influence what we do and how we do it. They also have an impact on how we feel. It's true we can't change all the things we dislike or that drive us crazy at work. But most of the time, we have a lot more control over what we do and how we do it than we think. Most importantly, we can always choose how we feel.

Assessing work fairly means monitoring how we see it, as well as how we see ourselves and others. For example, maybe you're trying to figure out what motivates your irritating boss, and you find yourself thinking: "She just wants money," or "He's a control freak," or "He doesn't have a clue." Instead, you may choose to see that your boss has human weaknesses as we all do but is trying to do the right thing. Or, instead of seeing your boss as incompetent, you see that she has huge pressures from above that are causing her to act in less-than-ideal ways.

What about your coworkers? Are they really all inept or evil? It's unlikely that they are. Instead of painting them with a broad brush, can you get a bit better at seeing them as individuals? You can also learn to diagnose why your team is working effectively— or why it is not. Again, this knowledge isn't a panacea. But it's a lot better than a monolithic, almost stereotypical view of people and teamwork.

And what's really going on in your organization? Is the culture as powerful and as toxic as you think it is? Are there any redeeming values that you can focus on? There usually are, and people have a hard time fighting you if you lead with something inspiring about the company, its noble purpose, and its values.

The basic lesson here is that if we want to assess our work situation fairly, we have to let go of the habitual ways we view people and our work experience. This new perspective doesn't fix the situation, of course, but it does help us to see more solutions than we had when we were locked into the old way of viewing things. The goal is to separate out what's you, what's them, and what's the organization. You can only change your own behavior, of course, but making these distinctions will help you determine whether you stay where you are or move on.

This is a big decision. I don't believe that making big changes is wise unless you know where you are going and how you might get there. So, to end this chapter, I invite you to spend time thinking about what really matters to you, the future you'd like to craft for yourself, the people you care about (at home and at work), and the kind of work life you'd like to have.

Stage Four: Run toward the Future, Not Away from the Past

When in dire straits, it's natural to want to run away from the problem. There are different ways of running away, of course. The most obvious is to quit your job. A not-so-obvious way is to shut down. We all know these people: they are physically present at work, but their minds and hearts are somewhere else.

Sometimes, of course, running away is the right thing to do, but it's better—much better—to run *toward* something. This requires you to engage in intentional change, a process of planning for the future developed by my good friend Richard Boyatzis.[23] You will have a chance to do this at the end of the chapter. For now, though, it's important to understand that when you've heard a wake-up call, you need to engage optimism and commit to a positive outlook about the future. Easier said than done, I know. But it's essential. Otherwise, you may make rash—even stupid— decisions that you may regret.

For intentional change to work, you also need to tap into confidence and self-efficacy. You may be beaten down. Your resilience and strength may be drained. But, as you see that glimmer of hope about the future, your belief in yourself will begin to grow. Trust yourself: if you've heard the call, and if you commit to moving toward a dream rather than running away, you are ready to craft a personal vision and a plan to get there.

Personal Reflection and Mindful Practice

Intentional change is a powerful process that will help you to move toward your dreams, while enjoying the journey. In this exercise, you will be guided to reflect on what's important to you now and in the future and gain clarity on what you want and where you are going. You will also have an opportunity to assess yourself, craft a learning plan, find people to help you, and consider how to practice new ways of engaging with life and work.

Each part of this exercise aligns with one of the five interrelated steps of intentional change:[24]

- Crafting a personal vision for my life and my work

- Seeing the truth of today: my real self

- Creating a learning plan

- Finding people who want to help

- Experimenting and practice

Crafting a Personal Vision for My Life and My Work

Begin by determining which aspects of your life are important to you, even those you may not spend a lot of time on now. Most people include things like family, love, health, spirituality, and work. Other people include friendships, making a difference, learning and growth, or living a comfortable life.

Next, think about how you'd like all of these aspects of your life to be in the future. Where do you want to live and with whom? What will you be doing? What kind of job or profession will you have? What kind of lifestyle will you have? What do you want your daily life to be like?

Now it's time to write. Imagine that it's five to ten years in the future. Pick a date that's significant to you, like a birthday, your child's graduation from school, and so on. Now put yourself in the future on that day—truly imagine that you are living the life you've dreamed about. Write as clearly as you can about each aspect of your life and work as it will be in the future. Write in the present tense, as if the future is already here. Be sure to include what will make you happier at work— what will make work feel meaningful, inspiring, and fulfilling.

This is your personal vision—an all-encompassing picture of the future that includes every aspect of your life. If you're worried that your dreams are far-fetched, remember that most of us are not in danger of dreaming too big. Far too often, we rein in our imagination too early and sell our dreams short.

Seeing the Truth of Today: My Real Self

The next step is to take stock. Where are you now? What strengths do you have that will help you bridge the gap between today and that future vision? What resources do you see in yourself, your immediate environment, or on the horizon? Of course, you will also want to think about what's missing. For example, do you need new skills or more education? Do you need a different social life or a new set of professional colleagues? Do you need to attend to your health and well-being?

To get an accurate sense of where you are today with respect to your work, ask others' opinions. You can do this in one of several ways: ask a few trusted friends at work; ask your partner or loved one what he or she thinks about your work life; get your coach's thoughts, if you're working with one. You can, of course, talk with your manager. But be careful. Often it's not safe to make yourself so vulnerable. Even if it is, your manager may have his or her own agenda in sharing feedback with you.

The bottom line is that you need multiple sources of information to get a clear picture of where you are now with respect to what's fulfilling at work and what's not, what you're good at that you'd like to continue, and what you need to change if you are to realize your vision for the future.

Creating a Learning Plan

The next step is to create a learning plan. This plan is more than performance goals and milestones; it is a plan for what you need to *learn or change* in order to reach your dream. Most learning plans include no more than five or six learning goals, each of which will take a year or more to attain. For example, maybe you see yourself reaching the executive suite in your company as part of your life vision. You're currently a middle manager who's come up through product development. You know you need to broaden your experience, so a learning goal might be: "Seek and attain a job in marketing and sales." Or, in your personal vision, you've written about living and working outside your home country. So, a learning goal could be to become fluent in another language. For each goal, you can now generate milestones and action steps—things you need to learn and do on your way to the goal.

Finding People Who Want to Help

Asking for help is not always easy, and finding the right people can be tough. They are there, though, and you will be surprised at how generous many of them will be when you ask for support.

Still, it's not always safe to ask for help from people at work. Just because you are on a path toward happiness and health doesn't mean others in your workplace are, and they may be resentful. If the culture is toxic, you have to watch out for how your request could be misconstrued or even used against you. Here are a few guidelines for finding your helpers and supporters:

- Don't start by asking people for help. Instead, identify a few people who have your best interests at heart and find ways to help *them*. They will welcome your generosity and want to support you in return.

- Tell these people that you are planning for a happier, healthier work life and that you need their help. Don't feel compelled to talk about your plan as you would a typical, conventional performance improvement plan. That's not what it is.

- Stay safe. Steer clear of those who could or would harm you to further their own agendas. You know who they are. So even if it would "look good on paper" to have that senior manager, or that mentor, as one of your helpers, if they won't have your best interests in mind, don't do it.

Experimenting and Practice

The next step is to make progress on your plan and learn along the way. You will need to take some risks, think differently, and behave differently, too. Keep two things in mind as you begin to try on a new attitude and new ways of approaching your work: make time for experimenting and be compassionate with yourself.

- MAKE TIME. If you try to add all of the actions in your learning plan to your already busy life, you will fail. You can't realize your personal vision unless you change how you spend your time. Here are some practical tips for changing your schedule:

  - Stop talking with people at work about how bad things are

  - Don't go to meetings you don't need to attend

  - Work at home at least once a week if you can; reduce your commute by going during nonpeak hours; even better, if it's a short distance, walk or bike to work

  - Learn to use technology better

  - Don't look at email or texts every hour (much less every ten minutes)

Remember, you're trying to make significant changes to how you live and work. This won't happen overnight, and you need to be a consistently active player. Stay connected to your dream and take the big and small actions that will help you to do things differently.

- BE COMPASSIONATE WITH YOURSELF. Few of us can enter a change process like this without tripping up and making mistakes. Be kind to yourself. Catalog wins and successes as you go. When you find yourself having a hard time learning or reaching a goal, focus on the learning, not the problems or stumbling blocks. And be brave.

CHAPTER 7

Sharing Happiness at Work

Create a Resonant Microculture on Your Team

Cultivating happiness at work is a deliberate, conscious act. You now know what it takes: finding and living your purpose, focusing passionately on your future, and building meaningful friendships.

There is one more thing you can do that will further increase your own happiness while also helping others: create a resonant microculture on your team. A resonant microculture is marked by a powerful and positive emotional climate as well as shared purpose, hope, vision, and norms that support happiness and success. Everyone is supported to work hard and work smart, while also feeling good about themselves and their accomplishments.

In this chapter I will talk about the kind of culture we all want at work and contrast it with the toxic cultures we see too often.

I will share ideas about what you can do to create a resonant microculture: take charge of the emotional climate of your team, commit to shared purpose and vision, and create emotionally intelligent norms to support healthy ways of working together. I will end the book with a happiness manifesto: actions we must all commit to if we are going to be happier and more successful at work.

The Power of Culture

Roberto Pucci is an executive vice president at Sanofi, a global health-care company.[1] He has also worked at Hewlett-Packard, Agilent Technologies, and Fiat. In each of these companies, he has revamped and transformed virtually all aspects of the people function. His innovations in talent management, leadership development, training, and benefits have shaped how people work and enabled employees and companies to excel. Throughout his career, Roberto has worked to humanize his organizations, making it possible for people to learn, grow, and thrive.

Roberto helps leaders create environments that support good work, good outcomes, and fun. His own meetings are focused and lively. People laugh a lot and they get things done, too. He sets the tone by telling jokes, as well as praising people and minimizing his own contributions. He's created a culture around him that diminishes hierarchy and supports creativity and innovation—a culture where the people who work for him feel empowered and committed.

Roberto said, "What drives me is the ability to make a difference in what I do. Every single time I left a job, I always asked myself, What is it that I'm leaving behind? If the answer ever turns out to be, 'Well, not that much,' then that would create a very deep sense of frustration. "And," he continued, "if my product is people, I want to leave the company with a better product. If, when I leave this job, I can say that the people who work at Sanofi are able to become better individuals because of what we do in this company, because of the way we manage and the relationships we've built, then I'm satisfied. That's what my job is all about."

One of the ways that Roberto has brought this to life has been to focus on culture, something he knows to be one of the most important drivers of individual and collective success. It can also be an almost insurmountable barrier. An organization's culture has an impact on virtually everything we say and do in the workplace: how we work; with whom we can talk and collaborate; what is taboo and what (or whom) is to be revered. Culture even has an impact on what we think and how and feel. Ultimately, culture affects the extent to which we can use our talents and whether or not we can be effective at work.

Unfortunately, too many of our organizations' cultures do not help us to accomplish our goals, much less be happy. They are toxic: they stifle talent, hijack success, and make us miserable. Resonant cultures are harder to find in our organizations; these are the ones that foster creativity, adaptability, and collaboration. It's easy to tell which is which.

Toxic Cultures

- Intense pressure to get short-term results

- Taboos against speaking up to power

- Us-versus-them mentality

- Dysfunctional competition

- Lots of talk about values but not enough action

- Lack of clarity around a vision

- Disrespect

- Lack of appreciation

- Pessimism

- Incivility and hurtfulness tolerated or even encouraged

- Inequity, absence of meritocracy, and injustice

These conditions result in fear, cynicism, lack of trust, anger, and withholding of time, energy, and talent, not to mention deep and pervasive unhappiness. Who wants to live that way at work?

What we need instead are resonant cultures where we can thrive physically, intellectually, and emotionally.[2]

Resonant Cultures

- A sense of unity around a noble purpose

- Overt commitment to virtues and values like honesty, forgiveness, gratitude, wisdom, and love

- A clear, inspiring, and shared vision of the future

- Generosity of time, talent, and resources

- Taboos against hurtful treatment of others, dishonesty, and cynicism

- Respect for the individual's right to grow and develop

- Celebration of differences

- Compassion and humane treatment of everyone in good times and bad
- Fairness and justice
- Integrity
- Fun

Resonant cultures help us to contribute to the organization's ultimate goals and to society. We delight in challenge, respect and appreciate one another's differences and strengths, and value generosity, openness, honesty, and justice. We are able to deal effectively with conflict without harming one another; we learn from our failures and revel in celebrating successes together.[3]

It's pretty obvious where most of us would prefer to work. But if your company isn't there yet, you can make it better, by taking responsibility for culture building.

Take Personal Responsibility for Your Culture

In *Primal Leadership*, Daniel Goleman, Richard Boyatzis, and I made the point that "great leaders move us. They ignite our passion and inspire the best in us."[4] Richard and I went on to say that "great leaders are awake, aware, and attuned to themselves, to others, and to the world around them. They commit to their beliefs, stand strong in their values, and live full, passionate lives."[5]

But it's not only senior leaders who must have these qualities and behave this way. Work is just too complicated and there's too much at stake to rely on a few people at the top of our organizations to guide us, help us to succeed, or make us happy. Today, *each and every one of us must be a resonant leader.* This is particularly true when we are talking about culture—that powerful force that affects how we feel, what we believe, and what we do at work.

Of course, it's nigh impossible for any one person to transform an entire organizational culture; it's just too complex and far-reaching. What you can do, however, is commit to creating a resonant microculture with the people you work with most closely: your office mates, peers, bosses, and team members.

You may work on or lead a formal team—a relatively stable group where each member has a designated role and goals are clear. Or, you may work on several teams that are less formal and more fluid—groups that come together around tasks or projects. You may not even be on a designated team. Instead, your group is the people you see and talk with every day, in person or online. Whatever the nature of your connection with others, you can take steps to create a healthier environment, no matter what else is happening in the larger company.

When you take responsibility for the culture that surrounds you and your closest colleagues, your team can become an oasis, even in the most dysfunctional organizations. Instead of a climate that is marked by tension, anxiety, and stress, your team can have an aura of excitement and camaraderie. Instead of questionable values and ethics, you and your teammates hold yourselves accountable for living shared values and behaving in ways that make you proud.

Creating a Resonant Microculture

If you want to create a resonant microculture, start by managing the emotional tone of your team—what it feels like to be at work. Next, focus on crafting a shared purpose that is rooted in values you all care about. Build a hopeful, shared vision that unites you as you look to the future. Last, commit to emotionally intelligent "rules of the game"—norms that make your team fun to be part of and more effective, too.

Shape Your Team's Emotional Reality

When we spend a good deal of time with the same people—as we do in teams—we create a shared *emotional reality*: the tone, tenor, and climate of the group. This happens because emotions spread like wildfire between and among people. And it's not that we are simply reading body language or encouraging one another to feel a certain way: our brains are wired to pick up and mirror other people's emotions. This means that moods are easily shared and the emotional reality on a team permeates every aspect of work.[6]

The emotional reality of a team is self-reinforcing: when one person's toxic feelings leak, others become negative, too. Shared fear, frustration, and cynicism breed more of the same. We find it very hard, if not impossible, to be happy when we are surrounded by misery.

The same is true for passion, hope, and caring: when people catch our positive feelings, they want to help, support, and be with us. People want to join us when we express commitment to meaningful values, excitement, enthusiasm, and hope. When we express warmth and acceptance for others, people can feel that too, and they like it.[7]

Happiness grows exponentially when we share it. The good news is that we have a great deal of control over the emotional reality of our team. To begin, it helps to reflect on how you typically influence your team's emotional reality.

Because so many organizations are unhealthy (or downright toxic), it is important to understand how your organization's culture affects you. You can easily get swept away by others or your organization's not-very-healthy climate. Instead, focus on what you find meaningful at work, consciously adopt a positive outlook, and focus on your own and others' strengths. This will go a long way to keeping toxicity at bay.

It is also important to get very good at managing your own emotions so you can contribute to building resonance with and for the people around you. Obviously, a healthy emotional climate will include a hefty dose of positive feelings. Excitement, enthusiasm, pleasure, pride, and joy, for example, are emotional experiences that constructively affect each person and a team's climate.

But anger, fear, frustration, and sadness have their place in the emotional reality of a team, too. These feelings signal injustice, danger, and inefficiency, among other things. Similarly, impatience, anxiety, and contempt are signs that something needs to change. We don't want to filter out all of these emotions. They are helpful markers that tell us that something's wrong and we need to do something about it. The trick is to know which feelings to share when, and how to do it in a way that fosters connection and collective well-being.

A powerful and positive emotional reality is supported by strong bonds among and between people. We often need to challenge ourselves to enter into relationships with our teammates that are more personal, caring, authentic, and intense than is common in most workplaces. This is scary for many people. But if you think about it, we already have very personal relationships at work. We just pretend we don't. Or, our relationships are charged and intense, but they are negative. We shy away from feelings that connect us—the kind of feelings that can make the emotional reality of our team more positive.

These shifts in your mindset and behavior can have an almost immediate impact on how it feels at work and can ultimately change the emotional reality of your team for the better. You can further build resonance by committing to a shared purpose—one that everyone on the team finds meaningful and compelling.

Seek Common Purpose

One of the most important pillars of a resonant microculture is a noble purpose borne of shared values and the desire to make a difference together. To create a shared purpose, we need to be clear about our own individual beliefs, our cherished principles, and our ethical code.

Next we need to find common ground. One way to do this is to look to the values that people the world over hold in highest esteem: justice, love, compassion, forgiveness, integrity, honesty, freedom, and wisdom, to name just a few. We can also look to the values our organizations uphold—values that we believe are noble and good and will help people strive to be their best selves. Almost all organizations have values that we can buy into—ones that make us proud to work at our company. True, most organizations are not perfect when it comes to acting on these values. We can, however, choose to adopt and live these values on our team.

We all come to work with different values and beliefs as a result of our different nationalities, religions, upbringing, and work experiences. So, people on our teams have personal values that matter to them—values that may not be understood or shared by everyone. Navigating this is not easy. It takes courage and emotional intelligence to have conversations that will result in shared purpose, but it's worth the effort. That's because these conversations help us discover common ground and foster stronger bonds among and between people.

A clearly articulated shared purpose enables us to focus our attention on something that matters to us, something we find meaningful. This is where walking the talk comes in. To bring shared purpose alive, we can help one another to do the things we love at work—things that make work feel like a calling. We can also make a point to appreciate one another for making a difference and celebrate successes.

A shared purpose is a powerful driving force in teams and a key aspect of your team's resonant microculture. So, too, is a vision of the future that inspires and motivates everyone.

Nurture Hope and Your Team's Shared Vision

Like shared purpose, hope is a pillar of a resonant microculture. The elements of hope—an optimistic vision of the future, plans for getting there, and the belief that we have the power to make it happen—are key to happiness and to our team's effectiveness. A clear picture of the future helps us to plan what we need to do and how to do it as a group. With a shared vision, we are emboldened to set noble goals that inspire us to challenge ourselves beyond what we thought possible.

Hope and a shared vision helps us to be effective as a team, to achieve and to excel. When we succeed or even face challenges together, we feel connected, committed, and inspired to give generously for the benefit of the group. When we know where we are going, roles become clearer, it is easier to see how to organize work processes and prioritize tasks, and we are willing to work hard together. Finally, shared hope helps us to feel stronger than we would alone and empowered to reach for our dreams.

To bring hope and a shared vision to your team, it's important to cultivate optimism, confidence, and adaptability. You can set the expectation that you will remain calm in the face of difficulties, be patient, and delay gratification.[8] These are examples of norms that support hope and shared vision on your team. There's more: to create and sustain a resonant microculture on your team, it is important for everyone to adopt norms that are grounded in emotional intelligence.

Commit to Emotionally Intelligent Team Norms

Emotional intelligence supports each of us to understand ourselves, what we care about, and our hopes for the future. Emotional intelligence also guides us in how we work together—how we create friendly, positive, and productive relationships.

Throughout this book, you have read stories of people who understand the power of purpose, hope, and friendships at work. All of these people also worked to create a resonant microculture in their workplaces. Here are some of the emotionally intelligent norms I've seen them foster on their teams:

- Seek to understand each other's viewpoints and feelings.

- Actively care for people.

- Respect and accept people for who they are.

- Connect with people around higher purpose and dreams.

- Engage in open, honest dialogue.

- Don't shy away from conflict, but don't harm people or relationships.

- Be reliable and consistent to build trust.

- Take the lead and also be a good follower.

- Celebrate success.

Emotionally intelligent teams also adopt norms that support a sense of belonging. One way to do this is to create a shared language—special ways of describing your work, your values, and your goals. Another way is to create team traditions and rituals— ways of celebrating success, for example, or things you always do to mark special occasions. You can also make it a habit to share playful times and fun. Sometimes the simple things matter most: talk *with* one another, not *at* one another; get to know each other personally; find something to care about and love in everyone.

These emotionally intelligent norms, along with shared purpose and a hopeful, shared vision, are key to your team's resonant microculture. By committing personally to taking responsibility for the culture and emotional reality of your team, your team can become a place where people can be effective and happy at work.

On the Road to Happiness

Life is too short to be unhappy at work. So, it's time to put into practice what you've learned. You can now liberate yourself from old-fashioned and flat-out wrong dictates about the nature of work. You can also free yourself from the happiness traps that keep you miserable: misplaced ambition, assuming money will make you happy, feeling helpless, and trying to do what others think you should do, rather than what you truly want. You can even begin to heal from the wounds of stress and overwork to make changes in your life and at work.

In place of these dangerous traps and old myths, you can choose to believe you have the right to be happy at work. This is where the journey begins, where you find and live your purpose, focusing passionately on your future, and building great friendships with your colleagues, bosses, and direct reports.

Happiness at Work: A Manifesto

- Be authentically yourself and celebrate others for who they are.

- Live the virtues and values that support purpose, hope, and friendships.

- Attend to and honor your feelings. Nurture positivity and optimism. Honor the pain of failure. Then, hold on to hope and rise.

- Celebrate and suffer *together*.

- Be calm.

- Be brave. Speak up to power so you can put purpose first and follow your dreams.

- Fight oppression. Insist on justice. Foster humane and enlivening working conditions. Protect yourself and others from dysfunction and toxic cultures.

- Break the rules about overwork; just don't do it anymore. Simplify everything you do. Work smart. Renew yourself through mindfulness practices, relationships, and joy.

- Be compassionate with yourself and others.

- Love yourself and find something to love and honor in everyone.

- Have fun.

EXPANDED TABLE OF CONTENTS

Chapter Two: The Happiness Traps
Myths That Hold Us Back

Chapter Four: The Power of Hope

Optimism Sparks Action

NOTES

Introduction

1. *How to Be Happy at Work* builds on and uses ideas and the extensive research I and my colleagues have conducted, as well as the practical work I have done with individuals, teams, and companies around leadership, culture, and organizational change. To read more of our earlier work, see Daniel Goleman, Richard Boyatzis, and Annie McKee, *Primal Leadership: Realizing the Power of Emotional Intelligence* (Boston: Harvard Business School Press, 2002); Richard Boyatzis and Annie McKee, *Resonant Leadership: Renewing Yourself and Connecting with Others Through Mindfulness, Hope, and Compassion* (Boston: Harvard Business School Press, 2005); and Annie McKee, Richard Boyatzis, and Frances Johnston, *Becoming a Resonant Leader: Develop Your Emotional Intelligence, Renew Your Relationships, Sustain Your Effectiveness* (Boston: Harvard Business Press, 2008).

2. Victor E. Frankl, *Man's Search for Meaning* (Boston: Beacon Press, 1959/2006).

3. Daniel Goleman was instrumental in turning the world's attention to emotional intelligence (EI) with his groundbreaking book, *Emotional Intelligence* (New York: Bantam Books, 1995). He, Richard Boyatzis, and I took the concepts to the business world with *Primal Leadership*. In this book, we made the case that EI was the foundation of excellent leadership. We followed with *Resonant Leadership* and *Becoming a Resonant Leader*. Both of these books demonstrate how EI supports outstanding personal effort, leadership, and organizational outcomes. Both also show how we can develop our EI. For research and findings on emotional intelligence and the relationship between emotional intelligence competencies and effectiveness, see Richard Boyatzis, "Competencies as a Behavioral Approach to Emotional Intelligence," *Journal of Management Development* 28, no. 9 (2009): 749–770; Richard Boyatzis, "Competencies in the 21st Century," *Journal of Management Development* 27, no. 1 (2008): 5–12; E. Amdurer et al., "Longitudinal Impact of Emotional, Social and Cognitive Intelligence Competencies on Career and Life Satisfaction and Career Success," *Frontiers in Psychology* 5, no. 1447 (2015): 1–15; and Richard Boyatzis, "Emotional and Social Intelligence," in *Encyclopedia of Management Theory*, vol. 1, ed. Eric Kessler (Thousand Oaks, CA: Sage Publications, 2013), 225–229.

Chapter 1

1. All of the stories and examples in this book are about real people. Many individuals and companies are named, with permission. In some cases, when material was sensitive, we decided to use pseudonyms and disguise the individuals and their companies. "Ari" is a pseudonym, as are all first names put in quotation marks when first introduced, throughout the book.

2. For a review of the effect of emotions on health, relationships, and workplace effectiveness, see Daniel Goleman, Richard Boyatzis, and Annie McKee, *Primal Leadership: Realizing the Power of Emotional Intelligence* (Boston: Harvard Business School Press, 2002); Richard Boyatzis and Annie McKee, *Resonant Leadership: Renewing Yourself and Connecting with Others Through Mindfulness, Hope, and Compassion* (Boston: Harvard Business School Press, 2005); Daniel Goleman, *Social Intelligence: The New Science of Human Relations* (New York: Bantam Books, 2006); and Daniel Goleman, *Destructive Emotions: A Scientific Dialogue with the Dalai Lama* (New York: Bantam/Random House, 2008). See also Julie Steenhuysen, "Anger Really Can Kill You, U.S. Study Shows," http://www.reuters.com/article/idUSN23265425, accessed September 2016. For the study this article is based on, see Rachel Lampert et al., "Anger Induced T-Wave Alternons Predicts Future Ventricular Arrhythmias in Patients with Implantable Cardioverter Defibrillators," *Journal of the American College of Cardiology* 9 (2009): 774–778.

3. David Sirota and Douglas Klein, *The Enthusiastic Employee: How Companies Profit by Giving Workers What They Want* (Indianapolis: IN: Pearson FT Press, 2013). See also Barbara L. Fredrickson, *Positivity: Top-Notch Research Reveals the Upward Spiral That Will Change Your Life* (New York: Three Rivers Press, 2009); and Gretchen Spreitzer and Christine Porath, "Creating Sustainable Performance," *Harvard Business Review*, January–February 2012, 93–99. For numerous articles on studies that support a positive workplace, see also Kim S. Cameron, Jane E. Dutton, and Robert E. Quinn, *Positive Organizational Scholarship: Foundations of a New Discipline* (San Francisco: Berrett-Koehler Publishers, 2003).

4. For information on the link between emotion, happiness, and success, see His Holiness the Dalai Lama, Archbishop Desmond Tutu, with Douglas Abrams, *The Book of Joy: Lasting Happiness in a Changing World* (New York: Avery, 2016); Spreitzer and Porath, "Creating Sustainable Performance"; Richard J. Davidson with Sharon Begley, *The Emotional Life of Your Brain: How to Change the Way You Think, Feel and Live* (London: Hodder, 2012); Shawn Achor, *Before Happiness* (New York: Crown Business, 2013); Shawn Achor, *The Happiness Advantage: The Seven Principles of Positive Psychology That Fuel Success and Performance at Work* (New York: Crown Business, 2010); David Rock, *Your Brain at Work: Strategies for Overcoming Distraction, Regaining Focus, and Working Smarter All Day Long* (New York: Harper Business, 2009); Martin E. P. Seligman, *Flourish* (New York: Atria Paperback, 2011); and Fredrickson, *Positivity*. For numerous studies and articles on the topics, see Shane J. Lopez, *Handbook of Positive Psychology* (New York: Oxford University Press, 2002); and

Richard J. Davidson, Klaus R. Scherer, and H. Hill Goldsmith, *The Handbook of Affective Science* (New York: Oxford University Press, 2003).

5. Candice Reimers, interview by author, February 2016.

6. I first heard this phrase from Nancy Ayon in a conversation she, Rebecca Renio, and I were having about the nature of happiness at work, and what pushes us over the line in one direction or the other.

7. My definition of happiness emerges from extensive study of the literature on the topic cited throughout this chapter coupled with my research on organizational culture and leadership practices around the world.

8. The body of literature linking positive emotions such as those associated with happiness with our effectiveness in life and at work is huge and growing rapidly. For an introduction and to read interesting studies and stories, see Sonja Lyubomirsky, *The How of Happiness: A New Approach to Getting the Life You Want* (New York: Penguin, 2007); Lahnna I. Catalino, Sarah B. Algoe, and Barbara L. Frederickson, "Prioritizing Positivity: An Effective Approach to Pursuing Happiness?," *Emotion* 14, no. 6 (2014): 1155–1161; Eric L. Garland et al., "Upward Spirals of Positive Emotions Counter Downward Spirals of Negativity: Insights from the Broaden-and-Build Theory and Affective Neuroscience on the Treatment of Emotion Dysfunctions and Deficits in Psychopathology," *Clinical Psychology Review* 30 (2010): 849–864; Tal Ben-Shahar, *Even Happier: A Gratitude Journal for Daily Joy and Lasting Fulfillment* (New York: McGraw Hill, 2010); Shane J. Lopez, Jennifer Teramoto Pedrotti, and C. R. Snyder, *Positive Psychology: The Scientific and Practical Explorations of Human Strengths*, 3rd ed. (Los Angeles: Sage, 2015); Bethany E. Kokl et al., "How Positive Emotions Build Physical Health: Perceived Positive Social Connections Account for the Upward Spiral Between Positive Emotions and Vagal Tone," *Psychological Science* 24, no. 7 (2013): 1123–1132; Boyatzis and McKee, *Resonant Leadership*; and Michael A. Cohn et al., "Happiness Unpacked: Positive Emotions Increase Life Satisfaction by Building Resilience," *Emotions* 9, no. 3 (2009): 361–368.

9. For interesting reading on happiness from a variety of philosophical and religious traditions, see Aristotle, *Nicomachean Ethics*, Oxford Classics, rev. ed., ed. Leslie Brown; trans. David Ross (Oxford, UK: Oxford University Press, 2009); His Holiness the Dalai Lama et al., *The Book of Joy: Lasting Happiness in a Changing World*; His Holiness the Dalai Lama and Howard C. Cutler, *The Art of Happiness: A Handbook for Living* (New York: Riverhead Books, 2009); The Dalai Lama and Rev. Robert Spitzer, S.J., "The Four Levels of Happiness," Catholic Education Resource Center, http://www.catholiceducation.org/en/religion-and-philosophy/apologetics/the-four-levels-of-happiness.html, accessed October 2016; Carol Glatz, Catholic News Center, "In recent interview, Pope Francis reveals ten top secrets to happiness," Catholic News Service, July 2014, http://www.catholiceducation.org/en/religion-and-philosophy/apologetics/

the-four-levels-of-happiness.html, accessed October 2016; David Belkovite, "Jewish Perspectives on Happiness," Eli Talks, http://elitalks.org/jewish-perspectives-happiness, accessed October 2016; Eckhart Tolle, *A New Earth: Awakening to Your Life's Purpose* (New York: Penguin 2005); Fariha Ullah, "The Concept of Happiness from the Islamic Perspective," http://www.academia.edu/1334559/Concept_of_happiness_in_the_Islamic_perspective, accessed October 2016; and "Happiness in Islam," part 2 of 3, https://www.islamreligion.com/articles/4322/happiness-in-i slam-part-2/, accessed January 2017.

10. For interesting reading on political stances on happiness as well as popular press, see "Constitution of the Republic of South Africa, 1996—Preamble," http://www.gov.za/documents/constitution-republic-south-africa-1996-preamble, accessed August 2016; "The Nordic Countries Are Probably the Best Governed in the World," *The Economist*, February 2, 2013, accessed September 2016; Elizabeth Gilbert, *Eat, Pray, Love: One Woman's Search for Everything Across Italy, India and Indonesia* (New York: Riverhead Books, 2006); Dan Harris, *10% Happier: How I Tamed the Voice in My Head, Reduced Stress Without Losing My Edge, and Found Self-Help That Actually Works—A True Story* (New York: Harper Collins, 2014); Daniel Goleman, *A Force for Good: The Dalai Lama's Vision for Our World* (New York: Bantam Books, 2015); and Gretchen Rubin, *The Happiness Project: Or, Why I Spent a Year Trying to Sing in the Morning, Clean My Closets, Fight Right, Read Aristotle, and Generally Have More Fun* (New York: Harper Collins, 2009), 69.

11. For works linking happiness and positivity to leadership and organizational health, see Spreitzer and Porath, "Creating Sustainable Performance"; Jane E. Dutton and Gretchen M. Spreitzer, *How to be a Positive Leader: Small Actions, Big Impact* (San Francisco: Berrett-Koehler Publishers, Inc., 2014); and Quinn, *The Positive Organization*.

12. Goleman et al., *Primal Leadership*; and Boyatzis and McKee, *Resonant Leadership*. For more on the power of positive emotions on leaders and organizations, see Quinn, *The Positive Organization*; Annie McKee, "Quiz Yourself: Do You Lead with Emotional Intelligence?," https://hbr.org/2015/06/quiz-yourself-do-you-lead-with-emotional-intelligence, accessed January 2017; Kim Cameron and Bradley Winn, "Virtuousness in Organizations," in *The Oxford Handbook of Organizational Scholarship*, ed. Gretchen Spreitzer and Kim Cameron, online, November 2012, http://www.oxfordhandbooks.com/view/10.1093/oxfordhb/9780199734610.001.0001/oxfordhb-9780199734610-e-018?mediaType=Article; Annie McKee, "The Emotional Impulses That Poison Healthy Teams," *Harvard Business Review*, July 2015, https://hbr.org/2015/07/the-emotional-impulses-that-poison-healthy-teams, accessed January 2017; Kim Cameron, *Practicing Positive Leadership: Tools and Techniques That Create Extraordinary Results* (San Francisco: Berrett-Koehler Publishers, 2013); and Fredrickson, *Positivity*.

13. For more on the power of positive emotions and their effect on leaders and organizations, see Quinn, *The Positive Organization*; Cameron, *Practicing Positive Leadership*; and Fredrickson, *Positivity*.

14. For thorough reviews of the field of positive psychology and information on the neuroscience of emotion, see Lopez et al., *Positive Psychology*; and V. S. Ramachandran, *The Tell-Tale Brain: A Neuroscientist's Quest for What Makes Us Human* (New York: W.W. Norton, 2011). See also Lois B. Murphy, *The Widening World of Childhood: Paths toward Mastery* (New York: Basic Books, 1962); C. R. Snyder and Shane J. Lopez, *The Oxford Handbook of Positive Psychology* (Oxford, UK: Oxford University Press, 2001); and Martin Seligman, *Authentic Happiness: Using the New Positive Psychology to Realize Your Potential for Lasting Fulfillment* (New York: Atria Paperbacks/Simon & Schuster, 2004).

15. For a review of the Sacrifice Syndrome, the physical and emotional state that arises over time as a result of stress, pressure, and negativity, see Boyatzis and McKee, *Resonant Leadership*, 35–55.

16. Ibid.; for more on the power of positive emotions and effectiveness as well as resonance in relationships, see Daniel Goleman and Richard E. Boyatzis, "Social Intelligence and the Biology of Leadership," *Harvard Business Review*, September 2008.

17. Quote is from Achor, *Before Happiness*, xiii; statistics are from Shawn Achor, "Positive Intelligence," *Harvard Business Review*, January–February 2012, 100–102; and Achor, *The Happiness Advantage*.

18. Achor, *Before Happiness*, xiii.

19. Emma Seppälä, *The Happiness Track: How to Apply the Science of Happiness to Accelerate Your Success* (New York: HarperOne/Harper Collins Publisher, 2016), 8.

20. For interesting studies and reviews on happiness and pro-social behavior, see Rubin, *The Happiness Project*; Susan A. David, Ilona Boniwell, and Amanda Conley Ayers, *The Oxford Handbook of Happiness* (Oxford, UK: Oxford University Press, 2014); Seligman, *Flourish*; and Frederickson, *Positivity*.

Chapter 2

1. *How to Be Happy at Work* emerged from an extensive review I have done on work I've conducted with leaders and in companies worldwide on practical issues many organizations face: leadership practices that can be improved; cultures that can be better crafted to support individual and collective success; and change processes that often fail to bring about optimal results. In addition, the conclusions I have drawn and the models presented in this work are built upon the foundation of earlier work done with my colleagues Daniel Goleman and Richard Boyatzis, as well as a host of other talented academics and scholar practitioners. To read more of our earlier work, see Daniel Goleman, Richard Boyatzis, and Annie McKee, *Primal Leadership: Realizing the Power of Emotional*

Intelligence (Boston: Harvard Business School Press, 2002); Richard Boyatzis and Annie McKee, *Resonant Leadership: Renewing Yourself and Connecting with Others Through Mindfulness, Hope, and Compassion* (Boston: Harvard Business School Press, 2005); and Annie McKee, Richard Boyatzis, and Frances Johnston, *Becoming a Resonant Leader: Develop Your Emotional Intelligence, Renew Your Relationships, Sustain Your Effectiveness* (Boston: Harvard Business Press, 2008).

2. Amy Adkins, "The Majority of U.S. Workers Not Engaged, Despite Gains in 2014," Gallup, January 28, 2015, http://www.gallup.com/poll/181289/majority-employees-not-engaged-despite-gains-2014.aspx), accessed July 2016; Amy Adkins, "Employee Engagement Stagnant in 2015," Gallup, January 13, 2016, http://www.gallup.com/poll/188144/employee-engagement-stagnant-2015.aspx, accessed September 2016; and Annamarie Mann and Jim Harter, "The Worldwide Employee Engagement Crisis," Gallup, January 7, 2016, http://www.gallup.com/businessjournal/188033/worldwide-employee-engagement-crisis.aspx, accessed September 2016.

3. In my work with thousands of leaders and their companies, I have consistently heard that the concept of "engagement" is, in a practical setting, linked with happiness at work, as I define it: experiencing work as purposeful and meaningful; having a clear and personally compelling vision of one's future; and warm, positive, friendly relationships with coworkers. The link between engagement and happiness is gaining traction in the academic community, too. See Martin Stairs and Martin Galpin, "Positive Engagement: From Employee Engagement to Workplace Happiness," in *Oxford Handbook of Positive Psychology at Work*, eds. Nicola Garcea, Susan Harrington, and P. Alex Linley (Oxford, UK: Oxford University Press, 2009).

4. For a review of Taylor's impact on management science, see Annie McKee, *Leaders: A Focus on Management* (New York: Pearson Prentice Hall, 2014).

5. For a thorough review of the importance of sleep to happiness and effectiveness, see Arianna Huffington, *The Sleep Revolution: Transforming Your Life, One Night at a Time* (New York: Harmony, 2016). See also Arianna Huffington, "Sleep Deprivation Is the New Smoking," *Huffington Post*, May 19, 2016, http://www.huffingtonpost.com/entry/arianna-sleep-smoking_us_573e3e27e4b0613b5129cf8e, accessed May 2016.

6. For information on overwork, see Sarah Green Carmichael, "The Research Is Clear: Long Hours Backfire for People and for Companies," *Harvard Business Review*, August 19, 2015, https://hbr.org/2015/08/the-research-is-clear-long-hours-backfire-for-people-and-for-companies, accessed January 2017. See also Neeru Paharia Belleza and Anat Keinan, "Research: Why Americans Are So Impressed by Busyness," *Harvard Business Review*, December 2016, https://hbr.org/2016/12/research-why-americans-are-so-impressed-by-busyness, accessed January 2017; Erin Reid, "Why Some Men Pretend to Work 80-Hour Weeks," *Harvard Business Review*, April 2015, https://hbr.org/2015/04/

why-some-men-pretend-to-work-80-hour-weeks, accessed January 2017; Silvia and Greg McKeown, "Why We Humblebrag About Being Busy," *Harvard Business Review*, June 6, 2014, https://hbr.org/2014/06/why-we-humblebrag-about-being-busy/, accessed September 30, 2016; and Lisa Evans, "Why You Need to Stop Bragging About How Busy You Are," *Fast Company*, April 21, 2014, http://www.fastcompany.com/3029294/work-smart/why-you-need-to-stop-bragging-about-how-busy-you-are, accessed September 30, 2016. For a thorough review of how and why we overfocus on work, to the detriment of health and happiness, see Arianna Huffington, *Thrive: The Third Metric to Redefining Success and Creating a Life of Well-Being, Wisdom, and Wonder* (New York: Crown, 2015).

7. Huffington, *Thrive*, 62.

8. Green Carmichael, "The Research Is Clear: Long Hours Backfire for People and for Companies."

9. For a comprehensive review of the impact of excessive focus on work, as well as the impact of defining success largely based on monetary and professional gains, and not personal health, well-being, or happiness, see Huffington, *Thrive*.

10. David McClelland, *Human Motivation* (Cambridge, UK: Cambridge University Press, 1988/2014).

11. Adam Grant, *Originals: How Non-Conformists Move the World* (New York: Viking, 2016).

12. Rachel Gillett, "How Walt Disney, Oprah Winfrey, and 19 Other Successful People Rebounded After Getting Fired," *Inc.*, October 17, 2015, http://www.inc.com/business-insider/21-successful-people-who-rebounded-after-getting-fired.html, accessed January 2017.

13. Jennifer Duvalier, interview by author, March 2016.

14. For more on emotional intelligence and emotional intelligence competencies, see Daniel Goleman, *Emotional Intelligence* (New York: Bantam Books, 1995); Goleman et al., *Primal Leadership*; Boyatzis and McKee, *Resonant Leadership*; McKee et al., *Becoming a Resonant Leader*; Richard Boyatzis, "Competencies for the 21st Century," *Journal of Management Development* 27, no. 1 (2007): 5–12; Daniel Goleman, *Social Intelligence: The New Science of Human Relations* (New York: Bantam Books, 2006). See also: R. E. Boyatzis et al., "EI Competencies as a Related but Different Characteristic than Intelligence," *Frontiers in Psychology* 6, no. 1 (2015); R. E. Boyatzis, J. Gaskin, and H. Wei, "Emotional and Social Intelligence and Behavior," in *Handbook of Intelligence: Evolutionary, Theory, Historical Perspective, and Current Concepts*, ed. Dana Princiotta, Sam Goldstein, and Jack Naglieri (New York: Spring Press, 2014), 243–262; and Shanil Haricharan, "The Impact of Emotional Intelligence on Public Leadership Performance in South Africa" (doctoral thesis, Stellenbosch University, 2015). To review alternative perspectives and research on emotional intelligence, see Peter Salovey and Daisy Grewal, "The Science of Emotional Intelligence," *Current Directions in Psychological Science* 14 (2005): 281–285;

David Mayer, Peter Salovey, and David Caruso, "Emotional Intelligence: Theory, Findings, and Implications," *Psychological Inquiry* 15 (2004): 197–215; David Caruso, David Mayer, and Peter Salovey, "Emotional Intelligence and Emotional Leadership," in *Multiple Intelligences and Leadership*, ed. R. E. Riggio, S. E. Murphy, and F. J. Pirozzolo (Mahwah, NJ: Lawrence Erlbaum Associates, 2001), 55–74; and David Mayer and Peter Salovey, "The Intelligence of Emotional Intelligence," *Intelligence* 17 (1993): 433–442.

15. For more on willpower, see Roy F. Baumeister and John Tierney, *Will Power: Rediscovering the Greatest Human Strength* (London: Penguin Books, 2011). For more on focus, see Daniel Goleman, *Focus: The Hidden Driver of Excellence* (New York: HarperCollins, 2013) and David Rock, *Your Brain at Work: Strategies for Overcoming Distraction, Regaining Focus, and Working Smarter All Day Long* (New York: Harper Business, 2009).

16. Contagious nature of emotions: during the past ten to fifteen years, there's been an explosion of research on how emotions are shared from one person to the next, one group to another. Much of this research is done in the field of neuroscience, including the groundbreaking work of Vilayanur Ramachandran, summarized well in V. S. Ramachandran, *The Tell-Tale Brain: A Neuroscientist's Quest for What Makes Us Human* (London: Norton & Co., 2011). See also Nicholas Christakis and James Fowler, *Connected: The Surprising Power of Our Social Networks and How They Shape Our Lives* (New York: Little, Brown, 2009); Goleman, *Social Intelligence*; Vijayalakshmi and Smanghamitra Bhattacharyya, "Emotional Contagion and Its Relevance to Individual and Organizational Behavior," *Journal of Business Psychology* 27 (2012): 363–374; Sigal G. Barsade, "The Ripple Effect: Emotional Contagion and Its Influence on Group Behavior," *Administrative Science Quarterly* 47, no. 4 (2002): 644–675; Jonas T. Kaplan and Marco Iacoboni, "Getting a Grip on Other Minds: Mirror Neurons, Intention Understanding, and Cognitive Empathy," *Social Neuroscience* 1, no. 3–4 (2006): 175–183; and Marco Iacoboni, "Imitation, Empathy, and Mirror Neurons," *Annual Review of Psychology* 60, no. 1 (2009): 653–670.

Chapter 3

1. This story is one of many from a project led by Dr. Monica Sharma, formerly of the United Nations. I feel deep gratitude to her and the team at the UN for the opportunity to do this important work in Cambodia, South Africa, Swaziland, and a host of Caribbean countries. Many thanks, too, to the talented team of faculty who worked on these projects, most particularly Edward Mwelwa.

2. Eckhart Tolle, *A New Earth: Awakening to Your Life's Purpose* (New York: Penguin, 2005); Thadeus Metz, *Meaning in Life* (Oxford, UK: Oxford University Press, 2016); Paul Rogat Loeb, *Soul of a Citizen: Living with*

Conviction in Challenging Times (New York: St. Martin's Griffin, 1999, 2010); Susan David, *Emotional Agility: Get Unstuck, Embrace Change and Thrive in Work and Life* (New York: Avery, 2016); Rick Warren, *The Purpose Driven Life: What on Earth Am I Here For?* (Grand Rapids, MI: Zondervan, 2013); Stephen Cahn, *Exploring Philosophy: An Introductory Anthology*, 5th ed. (Oxford, UK: Oxford University Press, 2014); Robert N. Bellah et al., *Habits of the Heart: Individualism and Commitment in American Life* (Berkeley: University of California Press, 1985/2007); Roy Baumeister, *Meanings of Life* (New York: Guilford Press, 1992); David Whyte, *River Flow: New and Selected Poems*, rev. ed. (Langley, WA: Many Rivers Press, 2015); and David Whyte, *Everything Is Waiting for You: Poems by David Whyte* (Langley, WA: Many Rivers Press, 2016).

3. Jeffrey Pfeffer and Robert I. Sutton, *Hard Facts, Dangerous Half-Truths, and Total Nonsense: Profiting from Evidence-Based Management* (Boston: Harvard Business Press, 2006), 66.

4. For interesting discussions of the prevailing tendency for our organizations and leaders to abdicate responsibility for ensuring that work is meaningful, see Rob Goffee and Gareth Jones, *Why Should Anyone Work Here? What It Takes to Create an Authentic Organization* (Boston: Harvard Business Review Press, 2015); Jane E. Dutton and Gretchen M. Spreitzer, *How to Be a Positive Leader: Small Actions, Big Impact* (San Francisco: Berrett-Koehler Publishers, 2014); Pfeffer and Sutton, *Hard Facts, Dangerous Half-truths, and Total Nonsense*; Gary Hamel, "Moonshots for Management," *Harvard Business Review*, February 2009; Daniel Pink, *Drive: The Surprising Truth About What Motivates Us* (New York: Riverhead Books, 2009); Kim Cameron, *Practicing Positive Leadership: Tools and Techniques That Create Extraordinary Results* (San Francisco: Berrett-Koehler Publishers, 2013); Kim S. Cameron, Jane E. Dutton, and Robert E. Quinn, *Positive Organizational Scholarship: Foundations of a New Discipline* (San Francisco: Berrett-Koehler Publishers, 2003).

5. There is a great deal of research as well as academic and popular writing on the impact of emotions on our ability to reason and tap into knowledge, creativity, and intelligence. Much of this work is summarized in Richard Boyatzis and Annie McKee, *Resonant Leadership: Renewing Yourself and Connecting with Others Through Mindfulness, Hope, and Compassion* (Boston: Harvard Business School Press, 2005), Daniel Goleman, *Social Intelligence: The New Science of Human Relations* (New York: Bantam Books, 2006); and Daniel Goleman, Richard Boyatzis, and Annie McKee, *Primal Leadership: Realizing the Power of Emotional Intelligence* (Boston: Harvard Business School Press, 2002). See also E. G. Mahon, S. N. Taylor, and R. E. Boyatzis, "Antecedents of Organizational and Job Engagement: Exploring Emotional and Social Intelligence as Moderators," *Frontiers in Psychology* 5 (2014); and Shane J. Lopez, Jennifer Teramoto Pedrotti, and C. R. Snyder, *Positive Psychology: The Scientific and Practical Explorations of Human Strengths* (Thousand Oaks, CA: Sage Publishing, 2015). For information on the neuroscientific linkages between

emotions, memory, and thought processes, see V. S. Ramachandran, *The Tell-Tale Brain: A Neuroscientist's Quest for What Makes Us Human* (New York: W.W. Norton, 2011). For concrete advice on how to develop emotional intelligence, see Annie McKee, Richard Boyatzis, and Frances Johnston, *Becoming a Resonant Leader: Develop Your Emotional Intelligence, Renew Your Relationships, Sustain Your Effectiveness* (Boston: Harvard Business Press, 2008).

6. Amy Wrzesniewski et al., "Jobs, Careers and Callings: People's Relations to their Work," *Journal of Research in Personality* 31 (1997): 21–33; Amy Wrzesniewski and Jane Dutton, "Crafting a Job: Reenvisioning Employees as Crafters of their Work," *Academy of Management Review* 26, no. 2 (2001): 179–201; Amy Wrzesniewski, Jane Dutton, and Gelaye Debebe, "Interpersonal Sensemaking and the Meaning of Work," *Research in Organizational Behavior* 25 (2003): 93–135; Katharine Brooks, "Job, Career, Calling: Key to Happiness and Meaning at Work?" *Psychology Today*, June 29, 2012, https://www.psychologytoday.com/blog/career-transitions/201206/job-career-calling-key-happiness-and-meaning-work. For more on Amy Wrzesniewski's and her colleagues' work, as well as the origins of this model, see B. D. Rosso, K. H. Dekas, and Amy Wrzesniewski, "On the Meaning of Work: A Theoretical Integration and Review," *Research in Organizational Behavior* 31 (2010): 91–127; Amy Wrzesniewski, "Callings," in *Oxford Handbook of Positive Organizational Scholarship* (Oxford, UK: Oxford University Press, 2012), 45–55; Brianna Barker Caza and Amy Wrzesniewski, "How Work Shapes Meaning," in *The Oxford Handbook of Happiness*, ed. Susan A. David, Ilona Boniwell, and Amanda Conley Ayers (Oxford, UK: Oxford University Press, 2013), chapter 52; and Bellah et al., *Habits of the Heart*.

7. Wrzesniewski et al., "Jobs, Careers and Callings"; Wrzesniewski and Dutton, "Crafting a Job"; Wrzesniewski et al., "Interpersonal Sensemaking and the Meaning of Work"; Amy Wrzesniewski, Justin M. Berg, and Jane E. Dutton, "Managing Yourself: Turn the Job You Have into the Job You Want," *Harvard Business Review*, June 2010, https://hbr.org/2010/06/managing-yourself-turn-the-job-you-have-into-the-job-you-want, accessed September 2016; Amy Wrzesniewski, "Job Crafting: Creating Meaning in Your Own Work," YouTube, https://www.youtube.com/watch?v=C_igfnctYjA, accessed January 2017; Jessica Stillman, "What You Can Learn About Job Satisfaction from a Janitor," *Inc.*, June 7, 2013, http://www.inc.com/jessica-stillman/what-you-can-learn-about-career-satisfaction-from-a-hospital-janitor.html, accessed March 2016; and David Zax, "Want to Learn How to Be Happier at Work? Learn How from these Job Crafters," *Fast Company*, June 6, 2013, http://www.fastcompany.com/3011081/innovation-agents/want-to-be-happier-at-work-learn-how-from-these-job-crafters, accessed September 2016.

8. Colin Browne, author conversations, 2016.

9. Wrzesniewski et al., "Managing Yourself"; Amy Wrzesniewski et al., "Job Crafting and Cultivating Positive Meaning and Identity at Work," *Advances in*

Positive Organizational Psychology 1 (2013): 281–302; Stillman, "What You Can Learn About Job Satisfaction from a Janitor"; Zax, "Want to Learn How to Be Happier at Work?"

10. Josh Peirez, interview by author, April 2016.

11. For a review of the original studies that upset the apple cart on extrinsic versus intrinsic motivation, see Edward L. Deci, Richard M. Ryan, and Richard Koestner, "A Meta-analytic Review of Experiments Examining the Effects of Extrinsic Rewards on Intrinsic Motivation," *Psychological Bulletin* 125, no. 6 (1999): 659.

12. Mark Lepper, David Greene, and Robert Nesbitt, "Undermining Children's Intrinsic Interest with Extrinsic Rewards: A Test of the 'Overjustification' Hypothesis," *Journal of Personality and Social Psychology* 28, no. 1 (1973): 129–137.

13. There are hundreds if not thousands of studies on what enables people to feel committed to their work, empowered, engaged, and intrinsically motivated. For reviews of various theories of motivation and the link to empowerment and engagement, see Annie McKee, *Management: A Focus on Leaders* (New York: Pearson Prentice Hall, 2014). For reviews of some of the best research, put into the context of today's environment, see Dan Ariely, *Payoff: The Hidden Logic That Shapes Motivation* (New York: Simon and Schuster/TED, 2016); Pink, *Drive*; Pfeffer and Sutton, *Hard Facts, Dangerous Half-truths, and Total Nonsense*; Carol Dweck, *Mindset: The New Psychology of Success* (New York: Ballantine, 2007); Goffee and Jones, *Why Should Anyone Work Here?*; Carol Dweck and Ellen Leggett, "A Social-Cognitive Approach to Motivation and Personality," *Psychological Review* 95, no. 2 (1988): 256–273. For a review of seminal studies, see Deci et al., "A Meta-analytic Review of Experiments Examining the Effects of Extrinsic Rewards on Intrinsic Motivation," 659.

14. Pink, *Drive*; Deci et al., "A Meta-analytic Review of Experiments Examining the Effects of Extrinsic Rewards on Intrinsic Motivation," 659; Boyatzis and McKee, *Resonant Leadership*.

15. Nikki Deskovich, interview by author, February 2016.

16. For extensive global research on universal values, see S. H. Schwartz, "Universals in the Content and Structure of Values: Theory and Empirical Tests in 20 Countries," in *Advances in Experimental Social Psychology*, vol. 25, ed. M. Zanna (New York: Academic Press, 1992), 1–65; and S. H. Schwartz, "Are There Universal Aspects in the Structure and Contents of Human Values?," *Journal of Social Issues* 50, no. 4 (1994): 19–45.

17. Mark McCord-Amasis, interview by author, May 2016.

18. Linda Loyd, "With $250M in 'Smart Labs,' Glaxo Consolidates U.S. Drug in R&D in Montco," Philly.com, November 8, 2016, http://www.philly.com/philly/business/20161108_With__250M_in__smart_labs___Glaxo_consolidates_U_S__drug_R_D_in_Montco.html, accessed

January 2017; Judy Packer-Tursman, "GSK Consolidates R&D with 'Smart Labs' in Philadelphia," PharmaDive, November 17, 2016, http://www.biopharmadive.com/news/gsk-consolidates-rd-with-smart-labs-in-philadelphia/430690/, accessed January 2017; Aimée McLaughlin, "GlaxoSmithKline Reveals New Smart Tech Research Space," Design Week, September 1, 2016, https://www.designweek.co.uk/issues/29-august-4-september-2016/pww-designs-glaxosmithklines-research-development-smart-space/, accessed January 2017.

19. GlaxoSmithKline website, http://www.gsk.com/en-gb/search/?q=mission, accessed April 28, 2016.

20. For more information on the role of mission in employees' search for meaning at work, see Goffee and Jones, *Why Should Anyone Work Here?*; and Pfeffer and Sutton, *Hard Facts, Dangerous Half-truths, and Total Nonsense.*

21. "Deepwater Horizon: Double, Double, Oil and Trouble," *The Economist*, April 18, 2015.

22. Dan Ariely, Emir Kamenica, and Dražen Prelec, "Man's Search for Meaning: The Case of Legos," *Journal of Economic Behavior and Organization* 67, No. 3–4 (2008): 671–677.

23. Duke Fuqua Business School, "What Managers Can Learn from Legos: Fuqua Professor Finds Business Lessons in Children's Toys," press release, November 14, 2008, http://www.fuqua.duke.edu/news_events/archive/2008/ariely_legos/#.V_llX5MrLdQ, accessed October 2016. See also Dan Ariely, "What Makes Us Feel Good About Our Work?" TED, April 2013, https://www.ted.com/talks/dan_ariely_what_makes_us_feel_good_about_our_work/transcript?language=en, accessed January 2017.

24. For perspectives on resonance in relationships and the impact of focusing on building strong, positive bonds at work, see McKee et al., *Becoming a Resonant Leader*; Boyatzis and McKee, *Resonant Leadership*; Goleman et al., *Primal Leadership*. See also Gretchen Spreitzer and Christine Porath, "Creating Sustainable Performance," *Harvard Business Review*, January–February 2012, https://hbr.org/2012/01/creating-sustainable-performance; Shawn Achor, "Positive Intelligence," *Harvard Business Review*, January–February 2012, https://hbr.org/2012/01/positive-intelligence; and Peter N. Stearns, "The History of Happiness," *Harvard Business Review*, January–February 2012, https://hbr.org/2012/01/the-history-of-happiness.

25. Adam M. Grant, *Give and Take: A Revolutionary Approach to Success* (New York: Penguin, 2013).

26. Matthieu Ricard, *Altruism: The Power of Compassion to Change Yourself and the World* (New York: Little, Brown, 2013). See also Lopez et al., *Positive Psychology.*

27. Cassie Mogilner, "You'll Feel Less Rushed If You Give Time Away," *Harvard Business Review*, September 2012, https://hbr.org/2012/09/youll-feel-less-rushed-if-you-give-time-away.

Chapter 4

1. Gina Boswell, interview by author, July 2016.

2. Nina Bahadur, "Dove Real Beauty Campaign Turns Ten: How a Brand Tried to Change the Conversation about Female Beauty," *Huffington Post,* http://www.huffingtonpost.com/2014/01/21/dove-real-beauty-campaign-turn s-10_n_4575940, accessed July 2016; and Katie Dupere, "Dove's New Campaign Challenges How the Media Portrays Women in Sports," Mashable.com, http://mashable.com/2016/07/26/dove-women-in-sports/#rWSwcYVBlqqR, accessed June 2016.

3. For classic articles and current research and press on anorexia and bulimia, see Ruth H. Striegel-Moore, Lisa R. Silberstein, and Judith Rodin, "The Social Self in Bulimia Nervosa: Public Consciousness, Social Anxiety and Perceived Fraudulence," *Journal of Abnormal Psychology* 102, no. 2 (1993): 297–303; R. A. Botta, "Television Images and Adolescent Girls' Body Image Disturbance," *Journal of Communication* 49, no. 2 (1999): 22–41; Alex Gregory, "Anorexia: The Impossible Subject," *New Yorker,* December 2013; M. D. Marcus and J. E. Wildes, "Eating Disorders," in *Cecil Medicine,* 24th ed., ed. L. Goldman and A. I. Schafer (Philadelphia: Saunders Elsevier, 2011); Randi Epstein, "When Eating Disorders Strike in Midlife", *New York Times,* July 13, 2009, http://www.nytimes.com/ref/health/healthguide/esn-eating-disorders-ess.html, accessed January 2017. For more information and resources on eating disorders, see New York Times Health Guides, http://www.nytimes.com/health/guides/disease/bulimia/overview.html, accessed September 2016; and National Eating Disorders Association, https://www.nationaleatingdisorders.org/, accessed January 2017.

4. Daniel Goleman, Richard Boyatzis, and Annie McKee, *Primal Leadership: Realizing the Power of Emotional Intelligence* (Boston: Harvard Business School Press, 2002).

5. Richard Boyatzis and Annie McKee, *Resonant Leadership: Renewing Yourself and Connecting with Others through Mindfulness, Hope, and Compassion* (Boston: Harvard Business School Press, 2005); and Goleman et al., *Primal Leadership.*

6. To read more about the impact of hope on our physiology and brain function, see Boyatzis and McKee, *Resonant Leadership.* See also C. R. Snyder, "Hope Theory: Rainbows in the Mind," *Psychological Inquiry* 13, no. 4 (2002): 249–275; Shane J. Lopez, Jennifer Teramoto Pedrotti, and C. R. Snyder, *Positive Psychology: The Scientific and Practical Explorations of Human Strengths* (Thousand Oaks, CA: Sage Publishing, 2015); and Shane J. Lopez, *Making Hope Happen: Create the Future You Want for Yourself and Others* (New York: Atria, 2013).

7. For reviews on current and classical research on hope, see Boyatzis and McKee, *Resonant Leadership*; Lopez, *Making Hope Happen*; Jerome Groopman, MD, *The Anatomy of Hope: How People Prevail in the Face of*

Illness (New York: Random House, 2004); C. R. Snyder, *The Psychology of Hope* (New York: Free Press, 1994); and Snyder, "Hope Theory: Rainbows in the Mind." For more on hope and how it fits into the broader field of positive psychology and the application of these ideas to organizations, see C. R. Snyder, *Handbook of Hope: Theory, Measures, and Applications* (San Diego, CA: Academic Press, 2000); Kim S. Cameron and Gretchen M. Spreitzer, *The Oxford Handbook of Positive Organizational Scholarship* (New York: Oxford University Press, 2012); Lopez et al., *Positive Psychology*; R. E. Boyatzis and K. Akrivou, "The Ideal Self as a Driver of Change," *Journal of Management Development* 25, no. 7 (2006): 624–642; A. Jack et al., "Visioning in the Brain: An fMRI Study of Inspirational Coaching and Mentoring," *Social Neuroscience* 8, no. 4 (2013): 369–384. For a practical look at hope and visualization, see Laura Vanderkam, "Why Visualization Isn't as Farfetched as It Sounds," *Fast Company*, January 2015, https://www.fastcompany.com/3040487/why-visualizing-success-its-as-far-fetched-as-it, accessed July 2015.

8. For information on how optimism is one component of hope, see Lopez, *Making Hope Happen*; and Boyatzis and McKee, *Resonant Leadership*.

9. On benefits of optimism, see Goleman et al., *Primal Leadership*; Boyatzis and McKee, *Resonant Leadership*; Carol Dweck, *Mindset: The New Psychology of Success* (New York: Ballantine, 2007); and Lopez et al., *Positive Psychology*.

10. For a discussion of optimism and pessimism as traits and learned abilities or perspectives, see Lopez, *Making Hope Happen*; Martin Seligman, *Learned Optimism: How to Change Your Mind and Your Life* (New York: Vintage, 2006). For a review of Seligman's and others' work on this topic, see Lopez et al., *Positive Psychology*.

11. For more on how our thoughts relate to optimism, see Lopez, *Making Hope Happen*; Sonja Lyubomirsky, *The How of Happiness: A New Approach to Getting the Life You Want* (New York: Penguin, 2007); Martin Seligman, *Authentic Happiness: Using the New Positive Psychology to Realize Your Potential for Lasting Fulfillment* (New York: Atria Paperbacks/Simon & Schuster, 2004); Seligman, *Learned Optimism*; and Karen Reivich and Andrew Shatte, *The Resilience Factor: How Changing the Way You Think Will Change Your Life for Good* (New York: Broadway Books, 2000).

12. See Thomas Suddendorf and Michael Carballis, "The Evolution of Foresight: What Is Mental Time Travel, and Is It Unique to Humans?," *Behavioral and Brain Sciences* 30 (2007): 299–351; Thomas Suddendorf, Donna Rose Addis, and Michael C. Corballis, "Mental Time Travel and the Shaping of the Human Mind," Royal Society Publishing, March 2009, http://rstb.royalsocietypublishing.org/content/364/1521/1317, accessed January 2017. For a review of Endel Tulving's and others' perspective on mental time travel, see Lisa Zyga, "Scientists Find Evidence for 'Chronesthesia,' or Mental Time Travel," PysOrg.com, December 22, 2010, http://phys.org/

news/2010-12-scientists-evidence-chronesthesia-mental.html, accessed May 23, 2016.

13. Lopez, *Making Hope Happen*.

14. Boyatzis and McKee, *Resonant Leadership*, 52.

15. Lopez et al., *Positive Psychology*; and Snyder, *The Psychology of Hope*.

16. Ibid.

17. Daniel Goleman, *Focus: The Hidden Driver of Excellence* (New York: HarperCollins, 2013).

18. American Psychological Association, "What You Need to Know about Willpower: The Psychological Science of Self Control," http://www.apa.org/helpcenter/willpower.aspx, accessed May 31, 2016; and R. Baumeister and J. Tierney, *Willpower: Rediscovering the Greatest Human Strength* (New York: Penguin Press, 2011).

19. Lechesa Tsenoli, interview by author, July 2016.

20. To read more about Lechesa's experience in detention, see Boyatzis and McKee, *Resonant Leadership*.

21. Gregg Easterbrook, *The Progress Paradox: How Life Gets Better While People Feel Worse* (New York: Random House, 2003).

22. Gregg Easterbrook, "When Did Optimism Become Uncool?," *New York Times*, May 12, 2016, http://www.nytimes.com/2016/05/15/opinion/sunday/when-did-optimism-become-uncool.html, accessed May 19, 2016.

23. Teresa Amabile and Steven J. Kramer, "The Power of Small Wins," *Harvard Business Review*, May 2011.

24. For a summary of research on the benefits and liabilities of goals and goal setting, see Annie McKee, *Management: A Focus on Leaders* (London: Pearson, 2014).

25. For an excellent guide for how to bring gratitude practices in your life, see Tal Ben-Shahar, *Even Happier: A Gratitude Journal for Daily Joy and Lasting Fulfillment* (New York: McGraw Hill, 2010). See also Martin E. P. Seligman, *Flourish* (New York: Atria Paperback, 2011); "In Praise of Gratitude," Harvard Health Publications, http://www.health.harvard.edu/newsletter_article/in-praise-of-gratitude, accessed January, 2017; David DeSteno, "Gratitude Is the New Willpower," *Harvard Business Review*, April 9, 2014, https://hbr.org/2014/04/gratitude-is-the-new-willpower, accessed January, 2017.

26. Annie McKee, Richard Boyatzis, and Frances Johnston, *Becoming a Resonant Leader: Develop Your Emotional Intelligence, Renew Your Relationships, Sustain Your Effectiveness* (Boston: Harvard Business Press, 2008).

Chapter 5

1. Janet Duliga, interview by author, February 2016.

2. For more on the impact of resonance on results, see Richard Boyatzis and Annie McKee, *Resonant Leadership: Renewing Yourself and Connecting with Others*

through Mindfulness, Hope, and Compassion, (Boston: Harvard Business School Press, 2005); Annie McKee, Richard Boyatzis, and Frances Johnston, *Becoming a Resonant Leader: Develop Your Emotional Intelligence, Renew Your Relationships, Sustain Your Effectiveness* (Boston: Harvard Business Press, 2008); and Daniel Goleman, Richard Boyatzis, and Annie McKee, *Primal Leadership: Realizing the Power of Emotional Intelligence* (Boston: Harvard Business School Press, 2002/2014).

    3. For research and commentary on happiness, relationships, well-being, and effectiveness, see His Holiness the Dalai Lama, Archbishop Desmond Tutu, with Douglas Abrams, *The Book of Joy: Lasting Happiness in a Changing World* (New York: Avery, 2016); Matthieu Ricard, *Altruism: The Power of Compassion to Change Yourself and the World* (New York: Little, Brown, 2013); Gretchen Spreitzer and Christine Porath, "Creating Sustainable Performance," *Harvard Business Review,* January–February 2012, 93–99; Barbara L. Fredrickson, *Positivity: Top-Notch Research Reveals the Upward Spiral That Will Change Your Life* (New York: Three Rivers Press, 2009); George E. Vaillant, *Triumphs of Experience: The Men of the Harvard Grant Study* (Cambridge, MA; London: Belknap Press of Harvard University Press, 2012); Robert E. Quinn, *The Positive Organization: Breaking Free from Conventional Cultures, Constraints, and Beliefs* (Oakland, CA: Berrett-Koehler Publishers, 2015); and Martin E. P. Seligman, *Flourish* (New York: Atria Paperback, 2011). See also Rob Goffee and Gareth Jones, *Why Should Anyone Work Here? What It Takes to Create an Authentic Organization* (Boston: Harvard Business Review Press, 2015); and Robert Sutton, *The No Asshole Rule: Building a Civilized Workplace and Surviving One That Isn't* (New York: Grand Central Publishing, 2007).

    4. David McWilliams, interview by author, February 2016.

    5. George Vaillant, in Scott Stossel, "What Makes Us Happy, Revisited," *The Atlantic,* May 2013, http://www.theatlantic.com/magazine/archive/2013/05/thanks-mom/309287/, accessed March 2016. There have been numerous scholarly articles and books published on the Harvard Grant Study over the years, as well as a number of pieces in the popular press. For a comprehensive review of the research and an interesting discussion of findings, see Vaillant, *Triumphs of Experience*; George E. Vaillant, *Aging Well: Surprising Guideposts to a Happier Life from the Landmark Harvard Study of Adult Development* (New York: Little, Brown, 2002); George Bradt, "The Secret of Happiness Revealed by Harvard Study," *Forbes,* May 27, 2015, http://www.forbes.com/sites/georgebradt/2015/05/27/the-secret-of-happiness-revealed-by-harvard-study/#590380ed2c9f, accessed October 2016; George Bradt, "Prime Genesis: Executive Onboarding for Better Results," October 2010, http://www.primegenesis.com/blog/2010/10/the-secret-of-happiness-per-harvard-class-of-1980/, accessed October 2016; and Joshua Wolf Shenk, "What Makes Us Happy?," *The Atlantic,* June 2009, http://www.theatlantic.com/magazine/archive/2009/06/what-makes-us-happy/307439/, accessed February 23, 2016.

6. Stossel, "What Makes Us Happy, Revisited."

7. For information on the Grant Study and other notable longitudinal studies looking at adult development, see Vaillant, *Triumphs of Experience*; and Vaillant, *Aging Well*. Specific studies cited by Vaillant as influential and important include a study of inner-city youth by Sheldon Gluck and Eleanor Gluck, *Unraveling Juvenile Delinquency* (New York: Commonwealth Fund, 1950); and a study of gifted children, both male and female, by Lewis Termin and Melita Oden, *The Gifted Child Grows Up: Genetic Studies of Genius*, vol. 4 (Stanford, CA: Stanford University Press, 1947). See also Kevin Leicht, ed., *The Wisconsin Longitudinal Study: The Class of 1957 at Age 65: A First Look; A Letter to Wisconsin's High School Class of 1957 and Their Families* (Madison, WI: privately printed, 2006); and Howard Friedman and Leslie Martin, *The Longevity Project* (New York: Hudson Street Press, 2011).

8. For information on the link between relationships and well-being, see Boyatzis and McKee, *Resonant Leadership*; Daniel Goleman, *Social Intelligence: The New Science of Human Relations* (New York: Bantam Books, 2006); Matthieu Ricard, *Altruism: The Power of Compassion to Change Yourself and the World* (New York: Little, Brown, 2013); Matthieu Ricard, *Happiness: A Guide to Developing Life's Most Important Skill* (New York: Little, Brown, 2006); Ed Diener and Robert Biswas-Diener, *Happiness: Unlocking the Mysteries of Psychological Wealth* (Malden, MA: Blackwell Publishing, 2008); John Capiocco, *Loneliness: Human Nature and the Need for Social Connection* (New York: W.W. Norton and Co., 2009); and Quinn, *The Positive Organization*.

9. For studies and reviews of research on the link between relationships and outcomes, see V. S. Ramachandran, *The Tell-Tale Brain: A Neuroscientist's Quest for What Makes Us Human* (New York: W.W. Norton, 2011); Tal Ben-Shahar, *Happier: Learn the Secrets to Daily Joy and Lasting Fulfillment* (New York: McGraw-Hill, 2007); Goleman, *Social Intelligence*; Fredrickson, *Positivity*; Richard J. Davidson, Klaus R. Scherer, and H. Hill Goldsmith, *The Handbook of Affective Science* (New York: Oxford University Press, 2003); Susan A. David, Ilona Boniwell, and Amanda Conley Ayers, *The Oxford Handbook of Happiness* (Oxford, UK: Oxford University Press, 2013); and Boyatzis and McKee, *Resonant Leadership*.

10. Sigal G. Barsade and Olivia A. O'Neill, "What's Love Got to Do with It? A Longitudinal Study of the Culture of Companionate Love and Employee and Client Outcomes in the Long-Term Care Setting," *Administrative Science Quarterly* 59, no. 4 (2014): 551–598. See also Sigal Barsade and Olivia A. O'Neill, "Manage Your Emotional Culture," *Harvard Business Review*, January–February 2016; and Sigal G. Barsade, "Employees Who Feel Love Perform Better," *Harvard Business Review*, January 13, 2014, https://hbr.org/2014/01/employees-who-feel-love-perform-better/, accessed March 8, 2016. For early research into this concept, see E. Hatfield, G. W. Walster, and E. Berscheid, *Equity: Theory and Research* (Boston: Allyn and Bacon, 1978); P. R. Shaver

et al., "Emotion Knowledge: Further Exploration of a Prototype Approach," *Journal of Personality and Social Psychology* 52, no. 6 (1987): 1061–1086; PubMed: US National Library of Medicine/National Institute of Health, https://www.ncbi.nlm.nih.gov/pubmed/3598857, accessed January, 2017; B. Fehr, "Prototype Analysis of the Concepts of Love and Commitment," *Journal of Personality and Social Psychology* 55, no. 4 (1988): 557–579; Beverley Fehr and James A. Russell, "Concept of Emotion Viewed from a Prototype Perspective," *Journal of Personality and Social Psychology* 60, no. 3 (March 1991): 425–438; and R. S. Lazarus, *Emotion and Adaptation* (Oxford, UK: Oxford University Press, 1991).

11. Barsade and O'Neill, "Manage Your Emotional Culture"; and Barsade and O'Neill, "What's Love Got to Do with It?"

12. See Shawn Achor, *The Happiness Advantage: The Seven Principles of Positive Psychology That Fuel Success and Performance at Work* (New York: Crown Publishers, 2010).

13. For information on the impact of stress on physical and mental health as well as workplace effectiveness, see C. Maslach, W. B. Schaufeli, and M. P. Leiter, "Job Burnout," *Annual Review of Psychology* 52, no. 1 (2001): 397–422; B. Buwalda et al., "Long-Term Effects of Social Stress on Brain and Behavior: A Focus on Hippocampal Functioning," *Neuroscience and Biobehavioral Reviews* 29, no. 1 (2005): 83–97; Robert Sanders, "New Evidence that Chronic Stress Predisposes the Brain to Mental Illness," *Berkeley News*, February 11, 2014, http://news.berkeley.edu/2014/02/11/chronic-stress-predisposes-brain-to-mental-illness/, accessed January 2017; David DiSalvo, "How Stress Affects Your Mental Health," *Forbes*, October 15, 2012, http://www.forbes.com/sites/daviddisalvo/2012/10/15/how-stress-affects-your-mental-health/#d3fc3df15e69, accessed January 2017; Kandi Wiens, "Leading Through Burnout: The Influence of Emotional Intelligence on the Ability of Executive Level Physician Leaders to Cope with Occupational Stress and Burnout" (PhD diss., University of Pennsylvania, 2016), via ProQuest, Publication #10158565; Shane J. Lopez, Jennifer Teramoto Pedrotti, and C. R. Snyder, *Positive Psychology: The Scientific and Practical Explorations of Human Strengths* (Thousand Oaks, CA: Sage Publishing, 2015); and Boyatzis and McKee, *Resonant Leadership*.

14. Candice Reimers, interview by author, February 2016.

15. For a comprehensive look at conformity and originality in the workplace, see Adam Grant, *Originals: How Non-Conformists Move the World* (New York: Viking, 2016).

16. Kenji Yoshino and Christie Smith, "Uncovering Talent: A New Model of Inclusion," Deloitte University, the Leadership Center for Inclusion, https://www2.deloitte.com/content/dam/Deloitte/us/Documents/about-deloitte/us-inclusion-uncovering-talent-paper.pdf, accessed March 2017; and Dorie Clark and Christie Smith, "Help Your Employees Be Themselves at Work," *Harvard*

Business Review, November 2014, https://hbr.org/2014/11/help-your-employees-be-themselves-at-work/, accessed January 2017.

17. Grant, *Originals.*

18. Goleman et al., *Primal Leadership*; and David DeSteno, "2 Ways to Regain Your Boss's Trust," *Harvard Business Review,* November 26, 2014, https://hbr.org/2014/11/2-ways-to-regain-your-bosss-trust, accessed March 2016.

19. Brian Uzzi and Shannon Dunlop, "Make Your Enemies Your Allies," *Harvard Business Review,* May 2012, https://hbr.org/2012/05/make-your-enemies-your-allies, accessed January 2017; Amy Gallo, "How to Respond When Someone Takes Credit for Your Work," *Harvard Business Review,* April 2015, https://hbr.org/2015/04/how-to-respond-when-someone-takes-credit-for-your-work, April 2015.

20. Adam Grant, *Give and Take: A Revolutionary Approach to Success* (New York: Viking Press, 2009); and Adam Grant, "In the Company of Givers and Takers," *Harvard Business Review,* April 2013.

21. Matt Egan, "5,300 Wells Fargo Employees Fired Over 2 Million Phony Accounts," CNN Money, September 2016, http://money.cnn.com/2016/09/08/investing/wells-fargo-created-phony-accounts-bank-fees/, accessed January 2017.

22. Amy Gallo, personal correspondence with author, March 2016.

23. Tiziana Casciaro, Francesca Gino, and Maryam Kouchaki, "The Contaminating Effects of Building Instrumental Ties: How Networking Can Make Us Feel Dirty," *Working Knowledge,* Harvard Business School, May 2014, http://hbswk.hbs.edu/item/the-contaminating-effects-of-building-instrumental-ties-how-networking-can-make-us-feel-dirty, accessed January 2017.

24. Ibid.

25. Rob Cross, Reb Rebele, and Adam Grant, "Collaborative Overload," *Harvard Business Review,* January–February 2016.

26. Ibid.

27. For information on laughter and positive emotions, see Shelley A. Crawford and Nerina J. Caltabiano, "Promoting Emotional Well-Being through the Use of Humour," *Journal of Positive Psychology* 6, no. 11 (2011): 237–252; Alison Beard, "Leading with Humor," *Harvard Business Review,* May 2014; "Laughter and Those 'Aha' Moments," Harvard Mahoney Neuroscience Institute, spring 2010, 2–10, https://hms.harvard.edu/sites/default/files/HMS_OTB_Spring10_Vol16_No2.pdf, accessed September 2016. For information on flow, see Mihaly Csikszentmihalyi, *Flow: The Psychology of Optimal Experience* (New York: Harper and Row, 1990).

28. Laura Vanderkam, "Will Half of People Be Working Remotely by 2020?," *Fast Company,* August 4, 2014, https://www.fastcompany.com/3034286/the-future-of-work/will-half-of-people-be-working-remotely-by-2020, accessed 2016.

29. Pamela Hinds, "4 Ways to Decrease Conflict Within Global Teams," *Harvard Business Review,* June 27, 2014, https://hbr.

org/2014/06/4-ways-to-decrease-conflict-within-global-teams, accessed October 2016.

30. Ibid.

31. Rebecca Knight, "How to Manage Remote Direct Reports," *Harvard Business Review*, February 10, 2015, https://hbr.org/2015/02/how-to-manage-remote-direct-reports, accessed October 2016.

32. Amy Gallo, "How to Deal with a Passive-Aggressive Colleague," *Harvard Business Review*, January 11, 2016, https://hbr.org/2016/01/how-to-deal-with-a-passive-aggressive-colleague, accessed October 2016.

33. Amy Gallo, "Dealing with Your Incompetent Boss," *Harvard Business Review*, June 6, 2012, https://hbr.org/2011/06/dealing-with-your-incompetent, accessed October 2016.

34. US Holocaust Memorial Museum, https://www.ushmm.org/information/about-the-museum, accessed January 2017.

35. National Alliance on Mental Illness, "Mental Health by the Numbers," http://www.nami.org/Learn-More/Mental-Health-By-the-Numbers, accessed January 2017.

36. Amy Gallo, "When You're Worried About a Colleague's Mental Health," *Harvard Business Review*, December 18, 2015, https://hbr.org/2015/12/when-youre-worried-about-a-colleagues-mental-health, accessed October 2016.

37. Boyatzis and McKee, *Resonant Leadership*; Goleman, *Social Intelligence*; and Goleman et al., *Primal Leadership*.

38. Karen Dillon, "Can You Be Friends with Your Boss?," *Harvard Business Review*, November 18, 2014, https://hbr.org/2014/11/can-you-be-friends-with-your-boss, accessed October 2016. See also Karen Dillon, *HBR Guide to Office Politics* (Boston: Harvard Business Press, 2014).

Chapter 6

1. I first heard this phrase from Nancy Ayon in a conversation she, Rebecca Renio, and I were having about the nature of happiness at work—and what pushes us over the line in one direction or the other.

2. Srikala (Kala) Yedavally-Yellayi, interview by author, March 2016. Kala's full title is Family Medicine Clerkship Director, Oakland University William Beaumont School of Medicine, and Osteopathic Family Medicine Residency Program Director.

3. Richard Boyatzis and Annie McKee, *Resonant Leadership: Renewing Yourself and Connecting with Others through Mindfulness, Hope, and Compassion* (Boston: Harvard Business Press School, 2005).

4. Ibid.

5. For discussions of the physiology of stress and its impact, see P. A. Thoits, "Stress and Health: Major Findings and Policy Implications," *Journal of Health and Social Behavior* 51, no. 1, supplement (2010): S41–S53;

S. J. Lupien et al., "Effects of Stress throughout the Lifespan on the Brain, Behaviour and Cognition," *Nature Reviews Neuroscience* 10, no. 6 (2010): 434–445; Kandi Wiens, "Leading Through Burnout: The Influence of Emotional Intelligence on the Ability of Executive Level Physician Leaders to Cope with Occupational Stress and Burnout" (PhD diss., University of Pennsylvania, 2016), via ProQuest, January 2017, Publication #10158565; Kandi Wiens and Annie McKee, "Why Some People Get Burned Out and Others Don't," *Harvard Business Review*, November 23, 2016, https://hbr.org/2016/11/why-some-people-get-burned-out-and-others-dont, accessed March, 2017; and "How Stress Affects Your Health," American Psychological Association, http://www.apa.org/helpcenter/stress.aspx, accessed January 2017. See also Shane J. Lopez, Jennifer Teramoto Pedrotti, and C. R. Snyder, *Positive Psychology: The Scientific and Practical Explorations of Human Strengths* (Thousand Oaks, CA: Sage Publishing, 2015); and Boyatzis and McKee, *Resonant Leadership*.

6. Thoits, "Stress and Health"; and G. Armon et al., "Elevated Burnout Predicts the Onset of Musculoskeletal Pain among Apparently Healthy Employees," *Journal of Occupational Health Psychology* 15, no. 4 (2010): 399.

7. Sarah Green Carmichael, "The Research Is Clear: Long Hours Backfire for People and for Companies," *Harvard Business Review*, August 19, 2015, https://hbr.org/2015/08/the-research-is-clear-long-hours-backfire-for-people-and-for-companies, accessed September 9, 2016; Arianna Huffington, *Thrive: The Third Metric to Redefining Success and Creating a Life of Well-Being, Wisdom, and Wonder* (New York: Harmony Books, 2015); and Arianna Huffington, *The Sleep Revolution: Transforming Your Life, One Night at a Time* (New York: Harmony, 2016).

8. For information on the importance of sleep, see Nick van Dam and Els van der Helm, "The Organizational Cost of Insufficient Sleep," *McKinsey Quarterly*, February 2016, http://www.mckinsey.com/business-functions/organization/our-insights/the-organizational-cost-of-insufficient-sleep, accessed January 2017; Arianna Huffington, *Thrive*; Nancy Rothstein, "The ROI of a Good Night's Sleep," *Huffington Post*, December 7, 2015, http://www.huffingtonpost.com/nancy-h-rothstein-/the-roi-of-a-good-nights-_b_8724282.html, accessed January 2017; "Lack of Sleep Costs Americans Billions of Dollars Each Year," *CBS News*, November 2016, http://www.cbsnews.com/news/lack-of-sleep-costs-americans-billions-of-dollars-each-year/, accessed January 2017; "Sleep Deprivation Leads to Symptoms of Schizophrenia, Research Shows," *Science News*, July 7, 2014, https://www.sciencedaily.com/releases/2014/07/140707121415.htm, accessed January 2017; and O. Van Reeth et al., "Physiology of Sleep (review)—Interactions between Stress and Sleep: from Basic Research to Clinical Situations," *Sleep Medicine Reviews* 4, no. 2 (2000): 201–219.

9. "Things You Should Know about Stress," National Institute of Mental Health, https://www.nimh.nih.gov/health/publications/stress/index.shtml,

accessed January 2017; Robert Sanders, "New Evidence That Chronic Stress Predisposes the Brain to Mental Illness," *Berkeley News*, February 11, 2014, http://news.berkeley.edu/2014/02/11/chronic-stress-predisposes-brain-to-mental-illness/, accessed January 2017; David DiSalvo, "How Stress Affects Your Mental Health," *Forbes*, October 15, 2012, http://www.forbes.com/sites/daviddisalvo/2012/10/15/how-stress-affects-your-mental-health/#d3fc3df15e69, accessed January 2017; J. Ciarrochi, F. P. Deane, and S. Anderson, "Emotional Intelligence Moderates the Relationship between Stress and Mental Health," *Personality and Individual Differences* 32, no. 2 (2002): 197–209.

10. "Depression in the Workplace," Mental Health America, http://www.mentalhealthamerica.net/conditions/depression-workplace, accessed February 3, 2016.

11. Arianna Huffington, *Thrive*, 28.

12. Boyatzis and McKee, *Resonant Leadership*.

13. For an interesting exploratory study on physician leaders' emotional intelligence and their ability to manage stress and avoid burnout, see Wiens, "Leading Through Burnout." See also Wiens and McKee, "Why Some People Get Burned Out and Others Don't" and Annie McKee and Kandi Wiens, "Prevent Burnout by Making Compassion a Habit," *Harvard Business Review*, May, 2017, https://hbr.org/2017/05/prevent-burnout-by-making-compassion-a-habit, accessed May 2017.

14. For information on overwork, see Green Carmichael, "The Research Is Clear." See also Neeru Paharia Belleza and Anat Keinan, "Research: Why Americans Are So Impressed by Busyness," *Harvard Business Review*, December 2016, https://hbr.org/2016/12/research-why-americans-are-so-impressed-by-busyness, accessed January 2017. See also Arianna Huffington, *The Sleep Revolution* and *Thrive*; Erin Reid, "Why Some Men Pretend to Work 80-Hour Weeks," *Harvard Business Review*, April 2015, https://hbr.org/2015/04/why-some-men-pretend-to-work-80-hour-weeks, accessed January 2017; Greg McKeown, "Why We Humblebrag About Being Busy," *Harvard Business Review*, June 6, 2014, https://hbr.org/2014/06/why-we-humblebrag-about-being-busy/, accessed September 30, 2016; and Lisa Evans, "Why You Need to Stop Bragging About How Busy You Are," *Fast Company*, April 21, 2014, http://www.fastcompany.com/3029294/work-smart/why-you-need-to-stop-bragging-about-how-busy-you-are, accessed September 30, 2016.

15. Richard E. Boyatzis, Annie McKee, and Daniel Goleman, "Reawakening Your Passion for Work," *Harvard Business Review*, April 2002, https://hbr.org/2002/04/reawakening-your-passion-for-work.

16. Boyatzis et al., "Reawakening Your Passion for Work."

17. For information on mindfulness, mindfulness practices, and the impact of mindfulness practices on health, well-being, and effectiveness, see Daniel Goleman and Richard J. Davidson, *Altered Traits*: *Science Reveals How Meditation Changes Your Mind, Brain, and Body* (New York: Penguin, 2017); Darren J. Good

et al., "Contemplating Mindfulness at Work: An Integrative Review," *Journal of Management* 42, no. 1 (2016): 1–29; Matt Lippincott, "A Study of the Perception of the Impact of Mindfulness on Organizational Leadership Effectiveness" (PhD diss., University of Pennsylvania, 2016); Jon Kabat-Zinn, *The Healing Power of Meditation: Leading Experts on Buddhism, Psychology, and Medicine Explore the Health Benefits of Contemplative Practice* (Boston: Shambhala Publications, 2013); D. C. Johnson et al., "Modifying Resilience Mechanisms in At-risk Individuals: A Controlled Study of Mindfulness Training in Marines Preparing for Deployment," *American Journal of Psychiatry* 171, no. 8 (2014): 844–853; E. A. Stanley and A. P. Jha, "Mind Fitness: Improving Operational Effectiveness and Building Warrior Resilience," *Joint Force Quarterly* 55, no. 4 (2009): 144–151; Matthieu Ricard, *Happiness: A Guide to Developing Life's Most Important Skill* (New York: Little, Brown, 2006); Jon Kabat-Zinn, Richard J. Davidson, with Zara Houshmand, *The Mind's Own Physician: A Scientific Dialogue with the Dalai Lama on the Healing Power of Meditation* (Oakland, CA: New Harbinger Publications, 2011); Jon Kabat-Zinn, *Full Catastrophe Living: Using the Wisdom of Your Body and Mind to Face Stress, Pain, and Illness* (New York: Delta, 1990); Daniel Goleman, *Destructive Emotions* (New York: Bantam Dell, 2003). See also Alina Tugend, "In Mindfulness, A Method to Sharpen Focus and Open Minds," *New York Times*, March 22, 2013, http://www.nytimes.com/2013/03/23/your-money/mindfulness-requires-practice-and-purpose.html, accessed January 2013; Ruth Wolever et al., "Effective and Viable Mind-Body Stress Reduction in the Workplace: A Randomized Controlled Trial," *Journal of Occupational Health Psychology* 17, no. 2 (2012): 246–258.

18. For an interesting study of the impact of mindfulness practices on emotional intelligence and leadership effectiveness, see Lippincott, "A Study of the Perception of the Impact of Mindfulness on Organizational Leadership Effectiveness."

19. Susan David, "Manage a Difficult Conversation with Emotional Intelligence," *Harvard Business Review*, June 19, 2014, https://hbr.org/2014/06/manage-a-difficult-conversation-with-emotional-intelligence, accessed October 2016.

20. Murray Wigsten, conversations with author, September 2016.

21. Charles Ramsey, conversations with author, September 2016.

22. For information on the Police Executive Leadership Institute, see https://www.majorcitieschiefs.com/pdf/news/2016_program_announcement.pdf, accessed March, 2017. For information on the United States Holocaust Memorial Museum, see https://www.ushmm.org, accessed March, 2017/. For information on the Major Cities Chiefs Association, see https://www.ushmm.org/, accessed March, 2017.

23. Boyatzis and McKee, *Resonant Leadership*; R. E. Boyatzis and K. Akrivou, "The Ideal Self as a Driver of Change," *Journal of Management Development* 25, no. 7 (2006): 624–642.

24. Annie McKee, Richard Boyatzis, and Frances Johnston, *Becoming a Resonant Leader: Develop Your Emotional Intelligence, Renew Your Relationships,*

Sustain Your Effectiveness (Boston: Harvard Business Press, 2008); Boyatzis and McKee, *Resonant Leadership*; Boyatzis et al., "Reawakening Your Passion for Work"; Boyatzis and Akrivou, "The Ideal Self as a Driver of Change."

Chapter 7

1. Roberto Pucci, interview and conversations with author, 2016.
2. For information on resonant cultures and cultures that support effectiveness and happiness, see Daniel Goleman, Richard Boyatzis, and Annie McKee, *Primal Leadership: Realizing the Power of Emotional Intelligence* (Boston: Harvard Business School Press, 2002/2014); Annie McKee, Richard Boyatzis, and Frances Johnston, *Becoming a Resonant Leader: Develop Your Emotional Intelligence, Renew Your Relationships, Sustain Your Effectiveness* (Boston: Harvard Business School Press, 2005); Richard Boyatzis and Annie McKee, *Resonant Leadership: Renewing Yourself and Connecting with Others Through Mindfulness, Hope, and Compassion* (Boston: Harvard Business School Press, 2005); Robert E. Quinn, *The Positive Organization: Breaking Free from Conventional Cultures, Constraints, and Beliefs* (Oakland, CA: Berrett-Koehler Publishers, 2015); Daniel Goleman, *A Force for Good: The Dalai Lama's Vision for Our World* (New York: Bantam Books, 2015); Rob Goffee and Gareth Jones, *Why Should Anyone Work Here? What It Takes to Create an Authentic Organization* (Boston: Harvard Business Review Press, 2015); Jane E. Dutton and Gretchen M. Spreitzer, *How to Be a Positive Leader: Small Actions, Big Impact* (San Francisco: Berrett-Koehler Publishers, 2014); Kim Cameron, *Practicing Positive Leadership: Tools and Techniques That Create Extraordinary Results* (San Francisco: Berrett-Koehler Publishers, 2013); Matthieu Ricard, *Altruism: The Power of Compassion to Change Yourself and the World* (New York: Little, Brown, 2013); and Jeffrey Pfeffer and Robert I. Sutton, *Hard Facts, Dangerous Half-truths, and Total Nonsense: Profiting from Evidence-Based Management* (Boston: Harvard Business School Press, 2006).
3. McKee et al., *Becoming a Resonant Leader.*
4. Goleman et al., *Primal Leadership*, 1.
5. Boyatzis and McKee, *Resonant Leadership*, 2005, 3. For more on resonant leadership, see Goleman et al., *Primal Leadership*; and McKee et al., *Becoming a Resonant Leader.*
6. For more on the contagious nature of emotions, see V. S. Ramachandran, *The Tell-Tale Brain: A Neuroscientist's Quest for What Makes Us Human* (New York: W.W. Norton, 2011); Boyatzis and McKee, *Resonant Leadership*; and Goleman et al., *Primal Leadership.*
7. Boyatzis and McKee, *Resonant Leadership*; and Goleman et al., *Primal Leadership.*
8. McKee et al., *Becoming a Resonant Leader.*

INDEX

ACKNOWLEDGMENTS

I've had times in my many years of work when I've been happy—ecstatic even—about my job. During those times, I felt my work was meaningful and that the future was bright. I loved the people I worked with, too (well, most of them). I've also had too many years when my work was a source of pain and stress. This book first emerged from the experiences I've had—both good and bad—with my own work. One thing I learned along the way is that life is too short to be unhappy at work—a major premise of this book.

Like me, most of us have good times and bad, but far too many people are unhappy at work. They feel stuck and alone. They want something more. And they know what they want and need at work.

So, to all the people I've met and worked with, and to those I work with today, thank you for your insights, knowledge, and keen understanding of what you—and all human beings—need in order to be fulfilled at work. Some of you are in big businesses, some of you are in government positions around the world, some of you are in NGOs, not-for-profits, and startups, and some of you work at home or in unconventional ways. It is your wisdom that I hope I have represented in these pages, and it is you I hope to honor.

In particular, I want to thank the thousands of people involved in the projects my team and I crafted to help us better understand leadership, organizational culture, and what people need in order to be effective at work. We learned so much together. In the thousands of interviews we held with employees, and in the deep studies of individuals' insights, wants, and desires, I began to sense that there was something more than met the eye—something more, even than the valuable thoughts about personal and organizational success. What I learned from this work is that underneath all the fancy words about leadership, effectiveness, and sustainable success are human beings—and our wonderful, mysterious, powerful human needs and aspirations. Every one of you—and I hope you remember me as well as I remember you—helped me to learn about happiness and about what really matters at work and in life.

I would like to express my deepest gratitude to the people who shared their stories, read drafts, and endorsed this book: Abhijit Bhaduri, Tony Bingham, Richard Boyatzis, Gina Boswell, Colin Browne, Nikki Deskovich, Janet Duliga, Jennifer Duvalier, John Fry, Adam Grant, Lynda Gratton, Marshall Goldsmith, Daniel Goleman, Arianna Huffington, Mark McCord-Amasis, David McWilliams, Nigel Paine, Gavin Patterson, Joshua Peirez, Roberto Pucci, Charles Ramsey, Candice Reimers, Ann Schulte, Martha Soehren, Lechesa Tsenoli, Nick van Dam, Murray Wigsten, and Srikala Yedavally-Yellayi.

This book could not have been written without the brilliant, talented, and fun team at Harvard Business Review Press, especially my incredible editors, Jeff Kehoe and Amy Gallo.

Jeff, working with you brings me joy. You bring out the best in me and help me find my voice, and for this I feel profound gratitude. You give me hope. You are a man of conviction, a man whose values drive decisions that will impact thousands of readers around the world. It is lovely to know that our friendship is at the very center of this book and that our thought partnership has once again flourished and borne fruit.

Amy, you are amazing and I love working with you! You are a gifted writer—your intellect and talent, your strong heart, and your incredible ability to find the diamond in even the roughest ideas have been so very important in crafting and writing this book. In all the work and writing we do together I feel supported, cared for, and challenged in the best way possible. I hope you know how much I care about you, value you as a person, and honor you as a professional.

Thank you, Laura Town, for our long and wonderful partnership and for your insightful, creative, and superb contributions to this book! Your talent as an editor is only surpassed by your brilliance as a writer. You are truly gifted. I am so grateful to be able to work with you, Karen Hoffman, Rachel Mann, and the team at Willtown Communications. Even more, though, I am grateful for our friendship. I treasure the journey we've been on over the years—our celebrations of joyous times and support during sad days has kept me going. You inspire me. My heartfelt thanks.

I would also like to express my gratitude to members of the Harvard Business Review Press editorial, design, and commercial teams: Sally Ashworth, Julie Devoll, Lindsey Dietrich, Stephani Finks, Sarah Green Carmichael, Curt Nickisch, Nina Nocciolino, Allison Peter, Keith Pfeffer, Dana Rousmaniere, Jon Shipley, Tim Sullivan, Kenzie Travers, Erica Truxler, and Jen Waring. In addition, thank you to Mark Fortier and Ken Gillett and your associates—because of you and your teams, this book will reach and help even more people.

To my friends at work and in life who have stood by me for so many years, who have shaped my thinking and supported my ideas, the words "thank you" aren't enough! I trust that you know what's in my heart: Bernice Bradley, Laurie Carrick, April Coleman, Niall FitzGerald, Ingrid FitzGerald, Jeff Frantz, Cordula Gibson, Pam Grossman, Shanil Haricharan, Frances Hesselbein, Frances Johnston, Yasmin Kafai, Dana Kaminstein, Jochen Lochmeier, Lezlie Lovett, Nigel Paine, Sharon Ravitch, Leslie Mancini Reed, Rona Rosenberg, Greg Shea, Kenwyn Smith, Kat Stein, Lindsay Tabaac and Jayce Park, Felice Tilin,

Christopher Allen Thomas, Cherish Tolentino, Lechesa Tsenoli, Liz Ulivella, Kandi Wiens, Stanton Wortham, Ben Wortham, Nyssa Worthington-Kirsch, and Chantelle Wyley.

My family is my rock. Thank you and I love you, Eddy Mwelwa, Rebecca Renio, Sean Renio, Sarah Renio, Andrew Murphy, Benjamin Renio, Murray Wigsten, Samantha Hagstrom, Matt Wigsten, Mark Wigsten, Rick Wigsten, Jeff Wigsten, Lori Wigsten, Mildred Muyembe, and Bobbie Renio. My love to their wonderful partners and children as well. And as ever, all my love, Erin Chroman.

ABOUT THE AUTHOR

Annie McKee, PhD, is a bestselling author, respected academic, speaker, and sought-after advisor to global leaders. She is a senior fellow at the University of Pennsylvania Graduate School of Education and has coauthored several groundbreaking books on leadership, including *Primal Leadership* (with Daniel Goleman and Richard Boyatzis), *Resonant Leadership* (with Richard Boyatzis), and *Becoming a Resonant Leader* (with Richard Boyatzis and Frances Johnston), all published by Harvard Business Review Press. These books and her many articles and blogs focus on the power of emotional intelligence to change how we lead and how we engage with our work. Now, in *How to Be Happy at Work: The Power of Purpose, Hope, and Friendship*, Annie shares wisdom and lessons learned from her decades of experience and research about what enables individuals and their teams to achieve sustainable, meaningful success.

Annie has advised many of the world's most influential leaders in sectors as varied as energy, media, health care, government, and nonprofits. Whether she is giving talks to business leaders, teaching executive doctoral students, working in provincial government offices in South Africa, or advising teams in the C-suite of *Fortune* 100 companies, Annie is committed to helping good leaders become great and to creating vibrant workplace cultures.

Annie has taken the road less traveled throughout her life, beginning her career as a community organizer. Then, upon completing her degree, Annie taught at a small college before joining the University of Pennsylvania's Wharton School. After a brief stint at a prominent consultancy, she took another risky step—leaving the security of a good job to found a consulting firm focused on developing values-based leadership and resonant organizations.

Today, as a senior fellow at the University of Pennsylvania Graduate School of Education, Annie continues to be guided by her belief that everyone, no matter who they are or what job they have, must be respected, honored, and encouraged to excel. In her work at Penn and beyond, Annie is committed to democracy and to encouraging every human being to seek happiness, health, and well-being. To this end, she supports positive social change in her role as a member of the Homeland Security Science and Technology Advisory Board and as a faculty member of the Police Executive Leadership Institute, a program she codesigned to support police executives in transforming their institutions to meet the needs of our complex cities and changing world.

Annie is married to Eddy Mwelwa, and they have four children and one grandchild: Rebecca, Sean, Sarah, Andrew, and Benji. Annie and Eddy live in Pennsylvania with their three dogs and two cats.